5/05

Hungary

Hungary

BY ANN STALCUP

Enchantment of the World
Second Series

Children's Press®

A Division of Scholastic Inc.

NEW YORK   TORONTO   LONDON   AUCKLAND   SYDNEY
MEXICO CITY   NEW DELHI   HONG KONG
DANBURY, CONNECTICUT

Frontispiece: View of Fishermen's Bastion after heavy snowfall

Consultant: Mihaly Szegedy-Maszak, Department of Central Eurasian Studies,
Indiana University, Bloomington, IN

Please note: All statistics are as up-to-date as possible at the time of publication.

Book production by Herman Adler Design

Library of Congress Cataloging-in-Publication Data

Stalcup, Ann, 1935–
  Hungary / by Ann Stalcup. — 1st ed.
        p. cm. — (Enchantment of the world. Second series)
  Includes bibliographical references and index.
  ISBN 0-516-23683-0
    1. Hungary—Juvenile literature. I. Title. II. Series.
  DB906.S73 2004
  943.9—dc22   2004008670

Hungary

Contents

Cover photo:
Man in traditional
Hungarian clothing

CHAPTER

Royal Palace

Crown of Saint Stephen

Vibrant Hungary

WHEN ONE THINKS OF HUNGARY, TWO THINGS IMME-diately come to mind: food flavored with paprika and wild gypsy violins. Both are so much a part of Hungary's vibrant culture, it would be impossible to visit the country without experiencing and enjoying both. But there is much more to Hungary than spicy food and a musical form that makes you want to kick off your shoes and dance.

Both the landscape and its history have shaped today's Hungary and the way its people live, work, and play. Hungary is a small, landlocked country, surrounded on three sides by mountains and bordered by seven other European nations. To some extent its mountain ranges have geographically isolated Hungary from its neighbors, perhaps making it easier for Hungary to retain its customs and costumes, its delicious foods, and its lively music.

Opposite: **Hungary's culture is one of vibrant food, dance, color, and people!**

The landscape of Hungary consists of fertile plains and rolling hills.

Much of Hungary's landscape consists of flat plains with fertile soil that is well irrigated by the Tisza and Danube, two major rivers that flow across the country from north to south. These plains are home to wheat and corn fields, fruit orchards, and other crops. On hilly ground, vineyards are a common sight. On the *puszta* (a word that once meant "wasteland," but now refers to grasslands), herds of horses and sheep roam under the watchful eyes of the *csikós*, Hungary's cowboys. The rural lifestyle that exists on the plains has changed very little over the centuries. People still work hard and live simply.

Hungarian cowboys, csikós, work together herding horses and sheep.

Hungarians are not concerned only with work. They love to play, too, and there are many recreation choices. Hungary is blessed with considerable underground thermal activity that has led to the creation of a large number of spas. The many thermal baths are always filled with people of all ages enjoying the benefits of a relaxing soak in the steaming medicinal water. Hungary's many lakes are also popular with holiday-makers. Huge Lake Balaton, known as the "Hungarian Sea," attracts both Hungarians and tourists to its shores for swimming, sailing, and bird-watching. An added attraction is the opportunity to sample the various fine wines that are produced around the lake.

The Danube River not only is beautiful, it is Hungary's main link to the outside world. Freighters are on the move constantly as goods are brought to and from Hungary on the Danube's long course from Germany to the Black Sea. Tourist boats are a

Tourist boats sail along the Danube, passing Budapest's Castle District.

common sight on the river. They bring visitors who are eager to experience Hungary's culture and history. Hungary welcomes its visitors with open arms by feeding them tasty paprika-enhanced dishes, entertaining them with gypsy orchestras, selling them decorative wooden pieces and colorful embroideries, and proudly showing off their most historic buildings.

While the Danube is Hungary's lifeline to the outside world, the vibrant city of Budapest represents, and links, the past and the present. It is a city with two faces: One is the much newer, bustling city of Pest, filled with busy streets, modern homes, and huge office buildings; on the opposite shore of the Danube is the city of Buda. Perched on a hilltop is Old Buda, a World Heritage site. Here, preserved in a small area, one can trace the city's history all the way back to Roman times. Again and again, over the centuries, buildings have been destroyed and new ones built on the same sites. What remains is a treasure trove of beautiful old homes, shady, steep cobblestoned streets, museums, a royal palace, and a medieval castle—a time capsule of Buda's often troubled past.

Over the centuries, Hungary has suffered many invasions. Frequently Hungary has been ruled by kings and dictators from other countries. But like the original founders of Hungary, their Magyar ancestors, today's Hungarians are a strong-willed and determined people. In spite of a long and troubled history, they have succeeded in retaining their unique language and cultural identity. The many minority groups that have been added to the mix have enriched Hungary's already rich culture.

Hungary's history as a state began in A.D. 896 when seven warlike tribal groups settled in the lowland region that is now Hungary. Since that time, Hungary has survived Mongol and Turkish invasions, domination by the German Hapsburgs, and then, in the twentieth century, forty-five years of communist rule. Its leaders have ranged from dictators to benevolent kings.

The Magyars, the name preferred by Hungary's residents, are an artistic, creative people. It is a culture that has produced well-known actors, play-wrights, and musicians, many of whom are people who have made the United States their home. Among the world's most prominent composers are three Hungarians: Franz Liszt, Zoltán Kodály, and Béla Bartók.

With great determination Hungary has retained the strong cultural heritage that sets it apart from its neighbors. In recent years, however, Hungary has been struggling between two worlds: the modern world enjoyed by much of the European community and its own ancient traditions. In large numbers young people and adults in search of higher wages, better living standards, and a more modern lifestyle have moved to the cities. Many of them now work in factories as Hungary moves toward industrialization. Others are involved in new businesses or in service industries.

National pride is a common trait among all Hungarians.

Hungary has become increasingly aware of its need to play a more active role in the European community. A decision was made that it would be beneficial for Hungary to join the European Common Market, which later would become the European Union, or the EU. But in order to be accepted as a member, certain requirements had to be met. Among those was the need for Hungary to have a truly competitive agricultural sector. Productivity was to be increased and a fair standard of living for the agricultural community was to be achieved. Hungary also had to be able to produce food at a reasonable price for consumers and be capable of moving goods freely within the EU.

In May 2004 Hungary officially became a member of the European Union along with its neighbors Slovakia and Slovenia, bringing the total to twenty-five. Neighboring Austria was already a member. Hungary plans to adopt the

Hungarians celebrate their country's membership into the European Union on May 1, 2004.

euro as its official currency in 2010. The EU has created a single Europe-wide market and strengthened Europe's voice in world affairs. It also supports cooperation among European people, works to raise living standards, and encourages the preservation of diversity. Hungarians have fought ardently for centuries to preserve their diversity. Membership in the European Union can only be beneficial to Hungary both financially and culturally.

From Mountains to Plains

H UNGARY IS A SMALL, LANDLOCKED COUNTRY. ON THREE sides it is surrounded by mountains: the Carpathians on the southeast and the Alps on the north and west. The country is sliced into three sections by the Tisza River and by the Danube River, a busy waterway that connects Hungary to its European neighbors on the north and south. One-fifth of Hungary's land is hilly. A small area is mountainous, but much of the country is covered by a low plain. Fourteen percent of the country is forested.

Lying near Europe's geographical center, Hungary is located in a low-lying basin known as the "middle Danube depression." Its people think of themselves as Central Europeans. Scenically, Hungary has something for everyone, no matter what their tastes or hobbies: mountains and forests for hiking, lakes for sailing and swimming, spas for relaxation, and the Danube for scenic boat trips.

Opposite: **Sunflowers reach for the sun near the Mátra Mountains.**

Most of Hungary's landscape is flat.

Hungary's Landscape

With an average elevation of less than 650 feet (198 meters), two-thirds of Hungary's land is almost completely flat. Its scenery is varied and ranges from rugged, forested mountain landscapes to

Hungary's Geographical Features

Highest Elevation: Mount Kékes, 3,330 feet (1,015 m) above sea level

Lowest Elevation: near Szeged, 259 feet (79 m) above sea level

Longest River: Tisza River, 360 miles (579 km) long

Largest Lake: Lake Balaton, 232 square miles (601 square km)

Largest City: Budapest, population 1,812,000

Highest Average Temperature: July, 71°F (21.6°C)

Lowest Average Temperature: January, 32°F (0°C)

Average Annual Precipitation: 26.4 inches (671 mm)

Greatest Distance East to West: 312 miles (502 km)

Greatest Distance North to South: 193 miles (311 km)

fertile plains and picturesque lakes. Around 51 percent of Hungary's land is under cultivation, a much larger proportion than is found in any other European country.

Hungary covers 35,919 square miles (93,030 square kilometers), 1 percent of Europe, an area about the size of the state of Indiana. It measures about 193 miles (311 km) from north to south and 312 miles (502 km) from east to west.

Since 1989, political changes have caused some of Hungary's neighbors to change their names and borders. Today Hungary shares its border with seven other European countries: Slovakia, Ukraine, Romania, Serbia and Montenegro, Croatia, Slovenia, and Austria. Although it is surrounded by so many different cultures and languages, it is much like an island. It remains remarkably untouched by its neighbors and their influences.

Hungary's Regions

Hungary is divided into three natural regions: the Great Plain (the Great Alföld), east of the Danube; Transdanubia, west of

The Danube River

The Danube, known in Hungary as the Duna, flows from north to south across Hungary's farmland. It slices the country in half before entering Serbia and Montenegro. The river serves as an important link with Hungary's trading partners. Day and night, boats ranging from barges to freighters to long, low, white tourist boats ply the Danube in both directions. Passenger ferries and hydrofoils speed between Budapest and Vienna from April to October when the river is free of winter ice floes.

At one time the Danube's twice-yearly flood seasons caused enormous damage to the farmlands and settlements in its path. Today, nearly 1,900 miles (3,057 km) of embankments have been built along the river. Irrigation channels ensure that the farmers have water for their crops.

With its islands and historic towns, the Danube Bend near Hungary's northern border is the country's most picturesque area. Dozens of holiday homes line its 14-mile (23-km) length. Two thousand years ago the bend formed the outer edge of the Roman Empire.

the Danube; and the Northern Highlands, which lie north of the Great Plain. These regions have been divided further to describe six geographic regions: The Great Plain, the Small Plain, Western Hungary, the Transdanubia Hills, the Transdanubia Mountain Range, and the Northern Highlands. The highest point in the country is the peak of Mount Kékes in the Mátra Mountains which rises to a height of 3,330 feet (1,015 m). The lowest part of the country lies in southern Hungary near Szeged in the valley of the Tisza River. Szeged, known as the paprika capital, is home to the spice most closely associated with Hungarian cooking.

The Great Plain (The Great Alföld)

Hungary's largest region, the Great Plain (Great Alföld) covers 50 percent of Hungary's land. Basically flat, the average height above sea level on the Great Plain is only 600 feet (about 183 m).

Five hundred years ago wild horses roamed the area and cattle grazed among the tall prairie grasses. In the sixteenth century, when the Turks destroyed most of the towns and cities in the region, once-productive farmland became a mosquito-infested swamp known as the puszta, which meant "wasteland" or "barren place" or steppeland.

Little by little the area has been reclaimed. The Great Plain is still referred to as the puszta, but the word has come to mean "farmland." The richest soil lies in the far southeastern section and today is a fertile plain much like the prairies of the United States. Large harvests of wheat have made the area Hungary's breadbasket. Hilly areas are covered with vineyards and fruit orchards. Where the land is salty and sandy, it is used for grazing sheep.

Although the region is used mainly for crops and cattle ranches, oil and natural gas are found in the southern section. At Hortobágy, 109 miles (175 km) east of Budapest, sections of the puszta have been preserved in their natural state and are now a national park.

The Small Plain (Kis Alföld)

Located in Hungary's northwest, the area known as the Kis Alföld is the second largest plain in the country but the smallest of its geographic regions. Together with the Great Plain, it accounts for two-thirds of Hungary's territory. It lies between the Alps and the Transdanubia Hills. Both the Danube and Drava rivers flow along the plain's borders, providing plenty of irrigation for its fertile farmlands.

The Kis Alföld is basically flat except along its western boundary where dense forests, streams, and rock formations cover the foothills of the Austrian Alps. Silt and sand deposits from the Danube River and its tributary, the Old Danube, have created rich farmland.

The Great Plain is Hungary's largest region where fertile soil produces grapes for wine making and wheat.

Southwest of the Small Plain is West Hungary. Stretching along the border with Austria, the region is also called the Lower Alps. It is here that the oceanic climate (from the Atlantic) has the most effect, causing the area to have the highest rainfall in the country.

West Hungary is a beautiful area. About one-fourth of it is forested, and much of the land is under cultivation, with over half of the region given to crops and vineyards.

A vineyard thrives in West Hungary.

Lake Balaton

During the Ice Age, a series of earthquakes divided the area into basins. Rainwater turned the basins into lakes and marshes. Wind, rain, and ice eroded the banks of each basin, gradually forming one large lake. Known as the Hungarian Sea, West Hungary's Lake Balaton is the largest lake in central Europe. It is 48 miles (77 km) long and 2 to 9 miles (3 to 14 km) wide. It covers an area of 232 square miles (601 sq km) and its average depth is 10 feet (3 m) deep. With its warm water fed in part by natural hot springs, it is a popular place for holiday homes. Foreign tourists are also drawn to the area by the beauty of the lake and the numerous resorts that surround the water. Spas, fed by hot springs, attract visitors seeking relief from their aches and pains. Lake Balaton, with its shimmering green color, reed beds, nearby forests, and hillsides terraced with vineyards, is a beautiful area. In the reed beds, known as wetlands, nesting birds, frogs, and fish find safe hiding places. Deer and wild boar feed in the oak and beech forests.

Lake Balaton is also a wonderful place for sailing. Although it is fairly shallow, the lake is large enough that waves and even white caps ruffle its green surface.

Transdanubia Hills and Mountains

The Transdanubia Hills cover the area west of the Danube, except for the Small Plain in the northwest. In southern Transdanubia, the hills stretch from the Zala River to the Dráva River and along Lake Balaton. The hills are home to oak forests, deep ravines, and clear mountain streams, making it a region of great beauty. Not only are there hills, the region also has the Mecsek and Villány mountains.

Looking at Hungary's Cities

Debrecen, Hungary's second largest city lies 145 miles (233 km) east of Budapest. When the Magyars arrived in the late ninth century, they found a colony of Slovaks living there. The Slovaks had named the region Dobre Sliem, "good soil," thus giving the town its modern name. As the city gradually developed, it built its wealth on salt, cattle, and furs.

Esztergom is a lovely flower-filled city located on the Danube across from Slovakia. Once a Roman settlement, Esztergom was Hungary's capital at the start of medieval times. Saint Stephen, Hungary's first king, was born in Esztergom and was crowned there in the year 1000. Esztergom Basilica (above) sits on a bluff high above the city. The largest church in Hungary, it is the administrative seat of the country's Roman Catholic Church. The Christian Museum there is one of the most important museums in Hungary.

The ancient town of Szeged, with its cobbled streets and its numerous horse-drawn carts makes you feel as if you had stepped back in time. Szeged is referred to as "the paprika capital" since it is famous for making paprika—the bright red spice that flavors many Hungarian dishes—and for its sausages and its sunshine—2,100 hours of it every year. The town has a lively intellectual atmosphere and has given birth to poets, writers, scientists, and famous schools.

Pécs dates back 2,000 years to Roman times when the town was known as Sopianae. It was also a center of early Christianity. A necropolis, a large ancient cemetery, was declared a World Heritage Site in 2000. Hungary's first university began here in 1367. Minarets and mosques are evidence of the Turkish occupation. One mosque in particular, the Pash Gazi Kasin (below), was built on the site of the first Roman temple and later a Catholic church. The mosque became a Christian church once again when the Turks left. The busy market town has steep streets and charming old houses. From the 1,735-foot (529-m) Misima Peak there are wonderful views of the surrounding area.

The Transdanubia Mountains stretch 124 miles (200 km) from Lake Balaton to the north all the way to the Danube River. Among the mountains in the region are the Bakony and Vértes ranges, areas rich in minerals.

Northern Highlands

The Northern Highlands form part of the Carpathian Mountain region of central Europe. The Highlands lie north of the Great Plain and stretch all the way to the Slovakia border. The mountains rise steeply from the plains below. Densely wooded mountains blanket the area, but skiing is popular in open areas of the forests.

Aggtelek National Park and the village of Josvafo can be found in the Northern Highlands.

The Northern Highlands are an area of dramatic scenic beauty. The landscape varies from stream-filled, forested mountain ranges formed from volcanic rock to the soft lime-stone of the Aggtelek and Bükk (Birch) Hills that are pocketed with huge cave systems and fantastic rock formations. Mount Kékes, in the Mátra Hills, is the highest peak in the country at 3,330 feet (1,015 m) high.

Rivers and Lakes

The country's longest river, the Tisza, flows 360 miles (579 km) from the northeast to the south through eastern Hungary.

The Szecheny Thermal Bath in Budapest is a popular spot for therapeutic bathing and a game of chess.

It empties into the Danube after it leaves Hungary. The Danube crosses seven European countries, forming part of Hungary's northern border before flowing north to south through the center of the country.

Hungary has over 1,000 lakes, the largest of which is Lake Balaton. Hungarians, as well as visitors from abroad, are attracted by the picturesque lakes and some 1,300 thermal springs popular for therapeutic bathing. Even Budapest, the capital, has many thermal baths. Thermal activity makes the earth below Hungary's surface hotter than it is elsewhere in Europe.

Hungary's Climate

Hungary lies where three climatic zones intersect: Atlantic (oceanic) to the west, Mediterranean to the south, and continental (Asiatic) to the east. The Atlantic climate is mild. The Mediterranean climate is hot and dry. The continental climate brings hot dry winds from the Russian steppes.

Hungary's weather is determined by which of the three climates prevails. Usually the climate is temperate, that is, pleasant and mild. Since the region is basically a flat basin, however, droughts are not unusual, particularly on the Great Plain, which has the greatest seasonal differences: cold, windy winters, and hot, dry, often stormy summers.

Hungary's hottest month is July, when temperatures average 60° Fahrenheit (16° Celsius). However, daily temperatures can go much higher. Budapest, in particular, is extremely hot and humid in the summer months. January, Hungary's coldest month, averages 36°F (2°C), although temperatures can drop much lower. The ground is often snow-covered and rivers and lakes are frozen over.

The flat region between the Danube and Tisza rivers has the most sunshine; the Lower Alps (the Alpokalja) and the northern mountains have the least. May, June, and July are Hungary's wettest months. The average annual precipitation is 24 inches (61 centimeters), although in the wetter western areas the precipitation can be as high as 32 inches (81 cm).

Natural Disasters

Hungary has had no earthquakes, blizzards, or hurricanes, but with its network of rivers and low-lying land, floods are frequent. One of the worst occurred on March 6, 2001, when the Danube burst its banks and flooded much of central Europe. Although more than ten thousand people were affected, miraculously no one died. Later the same year Hungary experienced "extreme temperatures." On December 10 the temperature dropped to -4°F (-20°C). Eighty-one people perished due to the unusually cold weather.

Plants and Animals

28

HUNGARY IS RICH IN WILDFLOWERS AND WILDLIFE, especially birds. As one of the most important stopping places for birds on their migratory route from northern Europe to North Africa, Hungary is a wonderful site for birders to observe a wide variety of birds. Of Europe's 395 species of birds, 373 have been sighted in Hungary.

Opposite: **In spring, storks arrive in Hungary to nest. This telephone pole suits these two just fine!**

The beautiful egret is a common sight in Hungary's wetlands.

A Birders' Paradise

Among the birds indigenous (native) to Hungary are waterfowl attracted by the many wetlands, lakes, and rivers. The most common birds are red-footed falcons, endangered imperial eagles, white-tailed eagles, corncrakes, spoonbills, aquatic warblers, great white egrets, great bustards, and saker falcons. In the Northern Uplands and the northeast, the arrival of numerous storks signals the beginning of spring. In addition to storks, other migratory birds that are seen on their route across Hungary are long-legged cranes and swallows.

The reeds of Hortobágy are a perfect place to spot waterbirds.

For birders, a visit to the Hortobágy region is a rewarding experience. Located on the Great Plain, Hortobágy is one of the best bird-watching sites in Europe. Over 334 bird species have been sighted there. The area is filled with saline (salty) steppe marshes and fishponds that attract large numbers of waterbirds. Lake Tisza, a man-made lake governed by Hortobágy National Park, is an area of reed beds and streams, a perfect habitat for many breeds of birds. There is always plenty to see in every season, though many migratory birds are seen in late summer.

Little Balaton, known locally as Kis Balaton, is a vast wetland. Its reed-choked ponds have been the breeding grounds of a hundred species of birds. Tiny Kányavári Island is the best spot for observing spoonbills, egrets, warblers, and terns. Particularly rewarding times to visit are April and August, when tens of thousands of migrating birds make this a place to stop and feed.

Wildlife Reserves and Protected Areas

Hungary has eleven national parks and almost one thousand protected areas, a large number for a small country. Families wanting to hike, picnic, or observe wildlife have a wide choice of locations.

Three parks are located on the Great Plain: Kiskunság, Krös-Maros, and Hortobágy. The parks, created to protect wildlife, also protect the fragile wetlands, marshes, and saline grasslands of the puszta.

In the Northern Uplands, one park is located in the Bükk Hills and the other is in the Aggtelek region (right) with its limestone karst formations, caves, and streams. Two additional parks are located along the Danube River and another is at Lake Balaton. The smallest park, at Fertó-Tavi, is shared with Austria. Two new parks were opened in 2002.

Not only do the parks serve as wildlife reserves, several have been designated as World Heritage Sites. The newest, designated in 2002, is the Tokaji Wine Region Cultural Landscape. Another is Hortobágy National Park. A third site is somewhat unusual, since it includes both buildings and landscape. Designated in 1987, it is listed as "Budapest, including the Banks of the Danube with the district of Buda Castle." The caves of the Aggtelek and Slovak Karst are shared with Slovakia.

To observe species other than waterbirds, such as owls, grouse, buzzards, and woodpeckers, two rewarding regions are Aggtelek, an area of hill karsts (limestone formations), and the Vértes Hills, a range of low wooded limestone hills west of Budapest.

Hungary has approximately 2,200 flowering plant species. Of these, 535 are protected, such as pheasant's-eye, and the wild peony found on the Great Plain, and the meadow anemone found in the Nyfrség. Some species are not normally found at this latitude, and others are normally seen only around the Mediterranean Sea. The most unusual of these is the Mediterranean hellebore found in the Mecsek Mountains. Many of Hungary's flowers, such as water lilies, buttercups, clover, foxgloves, daisies, and irises are found elsewhere in the world.

Several areas are home to rare and unusual flowers. In the Sárrét region, with its steppe, grasslands, marshes, and salt lakes, one might be lucky enough to find the early spider orchid, the variegated crocus, feather grass, and the pygmy iris. The marshy landscape of Kiskunság National Park has the Siberian iris, the slender sand iris, and several rare orchids such as the bug orchid, burnt orchid, and pyramidal orchid.

Foxgloves grow in abundance in Hungary.

Beech trees grow in Hungary's forests.

Hungary has a limited number of tree varieties. Most forest regions are filled with chestnut, beech, oak, and birch, trees common throughout Europe, as well as a small number of fir trees. Once, the Great Plains were wooded like the rest of Hungary, but, centuries ago, grazing animals brought by Asian invaders stripped the land. New trees that sprouted were promptly eaten by animals. Recently, in an attempt to reforest the area, reclamation projects involving irrigation and tree planting have begun.

The Puli Dog

A native of Hungary, puli (poo-lee) sheepdogs were first brought to Hungary by the Magyars one thousand years ago. Medium-sized, intelligent, light-footed, and fast, they are still used by shepherds and farmers for guarding and herding cows, pigs, and sheep. Using a series of bouncing movements, puli dogs leap across the backs of a herd in order to catch a runaway.

In appearance, pulis are quite unlike any other dog. Their long, thick, weather-resistant coats touch the ground; their eyes are completely hidden. Beneath the puli's outer coat the fur is soft and wooly. Gradually the two layers of fur tangle together to form long cords.

Hungary's Animals and Fish

Hungary was once home to more wildlife than it has now. As the animals' natural environment shrank through cultivation, so did their numbers. Only 10 to 15 percent of Hungary's land still has vegetation suitable for wild animals. Wild boars were once common, but as their habitat dwindled, and they were hunted, so did their numbers. Now they are found mostly in the Gemenc Forest.

In Hungary the wild boar is not as common as in the past due to overcultivation.

Today, boars, along with some species of deer, are protected as game animals. Lynxes and wolves may still exist in remote mountain regions. Wild horses that once roamed the puszta are gone. Herds of black buffalo, bred for their milk in the Lake Balaton region, now exist only in a small reserve.

Hungary's animals, such as foxes, squirrels, deer, bats, badgers, moles, hedgehogs, wolves, hares, wild boar, wildcats, beaver, and otters are found elsewhere in Europe. Today, of Hungary's 45,000 species, 855 are protected.

Since landlocked Hungary has no seacoast, the variety of fresh fish available in the nation is limited. The fish most commonly caught in Hungary's numerous lakes are carp, pike, catfish, perch, and bream.

Hungary's Colorful History

F OR THOUSANDS OF YEARS, PEOPLE HAVE LIVED ON THE LAND that is now Hungary. In the fifth century A.D., roaming Mongolian horsemen, led by their chieftain Attila the Hun, settled in the area. In spite of what you might think, the name Hungary does not have its origins in the word Hun. Instead, the name developed from the Turkish words *on ogur* or *onogur* meaning "ten arrows" or "ten peoples."

Árpád, leader of the Seven Magyar tribes

Hungary's history as a state began in A.D. 896 when seven Magyar tribes, led by Árpád, their *gyula* (chief military commander), migrated into the area now known as Hungary. It is believed that they came from the northeast, an Asian region between the Volga River and the Ural Mountains that later became Russia.

Hungary's Kings

Around 970 Géza, Árpád's great-grandson, became the new leader of the Magyars. He began organizing the tribes into one united nation. When he died, his son, Stephen (István in Hungarian) continued his father's work. Stephen chose Western Christianity (Catholicism) over Eastern Christianity (Orthodox), which linked Hungary

The Seven Tribes

The ancestors of the seven Magyar tribes lived in densely forested regions. They had limited skills as farmers and survived by hunting and fishing. In the fifth century, during the early Christian era, they first began migrating westward across the Urals. They adapted to their new environment by becoming herders. Bows and arrows were their only weapons. Their social unit was the clan, which was essentially an extended family. Each tribe consisted of a number of clans. Until Árpád (below on horse) was chosen to lead them on their westward migration in 896, tribal leadership had been hereditary.

The seven tribes settled in the lowland region bordering the Danube. They were a warlike people. For fifty years in the early 900s, these tribal groups raided one European city after another, taking slaves and causing considerable destruction. It wasn't until 955, when German King Otto I defeated the invading Magyars, that the raiding stopped.

to Western Europe rather than Asia, where the Magyars had their origins.

Stephen asked Pope Sylvester II to proclaim him king. The pope agreed, and in A.D. 1000 Stephen became Hungary's first king. Stephen made Roman Catholicism Hungary's official religion, and in 1083, forty-five years after his death, the Catholic Church made him a saint.

In 1241 Mongol armies invaded Hungary. Led by Batu Khan, the Mongols killed more than half the population. On the death of their ruler, in 1255, the invading armies withdrew, leaving much of the plundered country in ruins.

For three hundred years Hungary was ruled by Árpád's descendants. Under their leadership the country gradually recovered from the destructive Mongols. Although the Árpád dynasty ended in 1301 when their last king died without an heir, this period in history had established Hungary as a Christian country.

Hungary remained an independent kingdom for 225 more years. During this period one of the greatest kings was Charles Robert. A member of the Italian branch of the Anjou dynasty, he ruled Hungary from 1308 to 1342

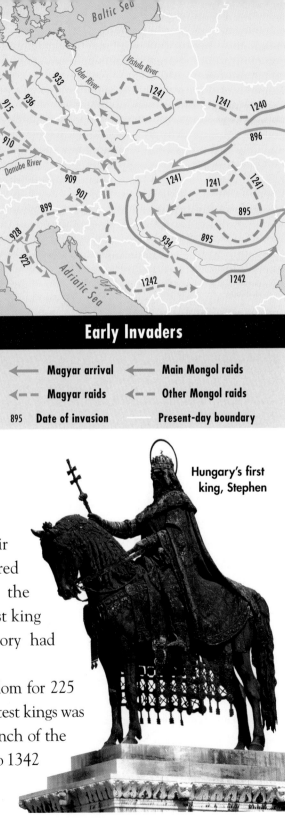

Early Invaders

← Magyar arrival ← Main Mongol raids

←-- Magyar raids ←-- Other Mongol raids

895 Date of invasion —— Present-day boundary

Hungary's first king, Stephen

King Matthias: Beloved Leader

Matthias (Mátyás), born in 1443 in Kolozsvár, Translyvania, was the second son of János Hunyadi, a legendary Hungarian general who, in defeating the Turkish army in 1456, prevented them from advancing into Western Europe. At that time there was considerable internal strife in Hungary, and when Matthias's older brother was murdered in 1458, fifteen-year-old Matthias was proclaimed king.

Matthias Corvinus organized a large, powerful, personal Black Army. To fund his army, he abolished tax exemptions enjoyed by important religious leaders, feudal landlords, and high-ranking noblemen. He protected the serfs, and improved the quality of life for those living in small towns.

Matthias valued architecture, the sciences, and all branches of the arts. He made Hungary an important cultural power in Europe and ordered the renovation of Buda's churches and monasteries. Under his leadership, Hungary became one of the most powerful nations in Europe. But when Matthias died, at age forty-seven, he had failed to accomplish his dream—that of banishing the Turks from Europe forever.

and brought peace to the country. Hungary had been plagued by civil conflict since the Árpád rule ended. By strengthening the monarch's power, Charles Robert decreased the power of the nobility by ousting those who were disloyal to him. He distributed their estates to his supporters. Charles Robert's son, Louis the Great (Louis I), added to Hungary's territory, but the land was lost after his death in 1382. His successor, Sigismund, failed to reclaim land lost in disputes or sold to repay debts. Sigismund became king in 1386 after marrying Mary, Hungary's queen. His reign lasted until 1437.

Since the mid-1300s, the Ottomans from Turkey had been advancing into Europe. In 1456 Hungarian nobleman János Hunyadi led the Hungarians in defeating the Ottoman Empire. In 1458 Hunyadi's son, Matthias Corvinus, became Hungary's king. Hungary prospered and became one of the centers of a widespread cultural movement known as the Renaissance.

King Matthias's death in 1490 brought more conflict to Hungary. A group of noblemen, known as the Diet, gained

Divided Hungary, 1569

- Kingdom of Hungary
- Ottoman Hungary
- Transylvania (Ottoman principality)

Above right: **This painting depicts the Battle of Mohács in 1526.**

considerable power. Hungarian peasants lived in miserable conditions, and as the noblemen's power increased, the peasants' lot became more wretched. In 1514 the peasants revolted, but they failed and became serfs (feudal tenant farmers), their lives little better than those of slaves.

Hungary Under the Ottomans

In the 1526 Battle of Mohács, Hungary was defeated by the Ottoman Empire. Already weakened by internal strife, the country quickly fell to the Ottomans (Turks). In 1569 Maximilian II, the Austrian Hapsburg ruler, signed a treaty with the Turks that divided Hungary into thirds. The north and west became the kingdom of Hungary. Eastern Hungary (Transylvania) became an Ottoman principality (a small state ruled by a prince). Central and southern Hungary remained under Turkish rule.

Life Under the Hapsburgs

In 1699 the Turkish sultan gave up his claim to Hungary when the Turks were expelled with the help of the Hapsburg emperor. By the early 1700s the Hapsburgs were in complete control of the country. Hungary became a province of the Austrian Hapsburg Empire, something the Hapsburgs had long wanted. They were harsh rulers. Their Counter-Reformation policies and heavy taxes alienated the nobility to a very great extent. Protestant regions of the country received the worst treatment, especially Transylvania where religious freedom was permitted and Protestant, Unitarian, and Catholic churches were all well established.

In 1703 Ferenc Rákóczi II, the son of a prominent family that included Transylvanian princes, led a nationwide uprising for independence. After eight years however, the Hapsburgs crushed the revolt, but then they did lessen the harsh political and economical conditions they had imposed on Hungary. In 1740 Hapsburg empress Maria

Portrait of Hapsburg empress Maria Theresa

Theresa began a forty-year reign. She caused widespread discontent by burdening the Hungarians with heavy taxes.

In the early 1800s Count István Széchenyi initiated many social and economic reforms. These helped restore Hungary's national identity. In the 1840s another patriot, Lajos Kossuth, emerged. The reform movement became a driving force for Hungarian independence. In 1848, with Austria's consent, the Hungarians established a government, although Hungary was still not completely free from Austria's control. Among the changes the Hungarians made was the granting of freedom for serfs.

Budapest's Royal Palace

Hungary has no royalty today, but Budapest's former Royal Palace can still be found on Castle Hill. Reached by a cable railway, the palace dominates the Buda skyline. The massive building, with its central dome, houses a complex of museums. These include the National Library and the National Gallery, which holds the country's largest collection of Hungaian works of art.

The first palace was built by King Béla IV, of the Árpád dynasty, in 1243. In the 1400s King Matthias added a Renaissance flavor to the architecture. Under Turkish invaders, it became army barracks. Then, in 1686, a Hapsburg-led attack almost destroyed the palace. In the 1700s the German Hapsburgs flattened what was left of the buildings, greatly increasing the height of the area. A massive, ornate baroque palace was built on top of the rubble.

During the 1944–1945 World War II siege of Budapest the palace was burned, but it has since been restored to its former splendor. Reconstruction work began in 1950 and continues to this day. To fully appreciate the size and splendor of the palace, it is best viewed from across the Danube River in Pest.

Although many things improved, such as freedom of the press, equality of worship, and the creation of a national guard, reforms were too gradual. Lajos Kossuth became head of a revolutionary Hungarian government that, in April 1849, declared its independence from Austria. It didn't last long. The Austrians, aided by Russia, defeated the Hungarian army only four months later, and Hungary was once again under Hapsburg rule.

Emperor Franz Joseph ruled both Hungary and Austria when Austria's stronghold weakened.

Austria-Hungary: A Dual Monarchy

Austria's power in Europe began to weaken. In 1859 Austria lost a war against France and Sardinia. In 1867 Hungary forced Austria's monarch, Emperor Franz Joseph, to give Hungary a dual monarchy—equal status with Austria. Franz Joseph ruled both countries. Military and foreign affairs were handled jointly. Each country's own government dealt with domestic decisions.

For fifty years both countries prospered. However, half of Hungary's population was made up of increasingly restless national groups. In the late 1800s and early 1900s the many demands of the Slovaks in northern Hungary, the Romanians in Transylvania, and the Serbs in Vojvodina, were ignored. Among these demands was the right to self-govern.

In 1914, a Serbian student and nationalist, Gavrilo Princip, from Bosnia-Herzegovina, assassinated Archduke Francis Ferdinand, heir to the Austro-Hungarian throne, and his wife. Austria-Hungary declared war on Serbia, and World War I began. The Central Powers (Germany, the Ottoman

Empire, Bulgaria, and Austria-Hungary) fought against the allied Armed Forces, or the Allies (France, Russia, Great Britain, Serbia, Belgium, Italy, and other countries). In 1917 the United States joined the Allies. The war ended when Austria-Hungary surrendered on November 4, 1918, after the Italian victory at Vittoro Veneto. The Allies and the Central Powers signed an armistice agreement on November 11. An armistice means that warring parties agree to suspend hostilities.

On October 31, 1918, just days before World War I ended, the Hungarian people revolted, declaring Hungary a republic and Count Mihály Károlyi their president. When a coalition government was formed between Communists and Socialists in March 1919, Károlyi resigned and Béla Kun, the Communist leader, took control as dictator. Soon Romania began to harass

Below right: **Admiral Miklós Horthy, head of Hungary's government from 1919 to 1944**

Adriatic Sea

Mediterranean Sea

Hungary After World War I

Austria-Hungary, 1914

Kingdom of Hungary, 1914

Hungary, 1920–1938, 1945–present

Hungary, 1938–1945

—— Present-day boundaries

Budapest

Hungary's borders. Unable to defend Hungary against the attacks, Kun's rule lasted only 133 days. Romania occupied much of Hungary. The year 1919 was filled with turmoil. Late in the year Admiral Miklós Horthy created a monarchy, naming himself regent of Hungary and leader of a conservative government. His leadership lasted twenty-five years.

As part of the 1920 World War I peace settlements between Hungary and the Allies, the Treaty of Trianon took away more than two-thirds of Hungary's land. Over half of Hungary's prewar population and one-third of Hungary's ethnic people now lived outside Hungary's borders. Hungarian land became parts of Romania, Austria, Czechoslovakia, and the Kingdom of the Serbs, Croats, and Slovenes (later called Yugoslavia). Since then, Hungary's borders have changed very little.

The Rise of Nazi Germany

In the 1930s, when Germany's Nazi party, under the leadership of Adolf Hitler, rose to power, they promised Hungary that some of the territory lost under the Treaty of Trianon would be returned. Thus in 1938 Hungary regained parts of Yugoslavia, Romania, and Czechoslovakia. In exchange, in 1941, two years after the start of World War II in Europe, Hungary assisted Hitler in attacking Yugoslavia, becoming one of the Axis countries fighting against Britain, France, and the other Allies.

In 1943 Hitler decided he no longer trusted Hungary because the president withdrew troops after heavy losses in fighting the Soviets. Hitler feared that Hungary might sign a separate peace agreement. After seizing control of the country in

Cardinal József Mindszenty, Hungarian Hero

József Mindszenty was bishop of Veszprém during the German occupation of Hungary in World War II. A brave man, he made no secret of his anti-German feelings, and the Hungarian government imprisoned him for several months. After the war he became archbishop of Esztergom and Catholic primate of Hungary. In 1946, as cardinal, he publicly showed his opposition to communism.

In 1948 Mindszenty was arrested on a variety of charges, including treason. He pleaded guilty to most charges but was believed to have been drugged before confessing. The court sentenced him to life imprisonment, but he was freed by rebels during the 1956 uprising (left). Taking refuge in the American Embassy in Budapest, he refused to leave Hungary unless the government pardoned him. In 1971 the Vatican and the Hungarian government came to an agreement and the cardinal settled in Austria. Anxious to improve relations with Hungary, Pope Paul VI removed Mindszenty from his position as primate of Hungary.

March 1944, Hitler shipped more than half a million Hungarian Jews and Gypsies to concentration camps. Most of them died there. In late 1944 the Soviet Union invaded Hungary. Hungary and the Soviets signed an armistice in January 1945, with Hungary agreeing once again to give up the territory it had regained in 1938.

Hungary and Communism

World War II ended in Europe in May 1945, when the German surrender was signed. The last German troops had been driven out of Hungary on April 4, 1945. During the November elections a coalition government was formed, and in the economic and social reforms that followed, land was given to peasants. The Smallholder Party earned a majority of the election votes. They had emerged after World War I, advocating land reform. However, the Communists gradually gained control due largely to the continued presence of Soviet troops in Hungary. Hungary became the Hungarian People's Republic.

More elections were held in 1947. The Communists failed to win a majority of the votes, but party members held enough key government positions to enable them to tighten their squeeze of the Hungarian people. The 1949 constitution was modeled after that of the Soviet Union, and the Communist Party became the country's only legal party—opposition parties were not allowed.

Everything began to change. Before World War II, Hungary had been mainly an agricultural country. With the Communists in control, many farms and industries were taken over. Hungary became increasingly industrialized, and people left rural communities to work where industries needed workers. It was soon evident that the Communists could not meet their production goals. Even farm production fell behind.

Much farmland was still privately owned. The rest had become state farms or collective farms. On collective farms, groups of families worked together, owning some of the land

Hungarian farmers on a state farm.

By signing a declaration, countries in Eastern Europe became members of the Warsaw Pact. This signing took place in Czechoslovakia in 1956.

and equipment themselves. They were given a wage and a portion of the farm's earnings. State farms were managed by a director and laborers earned a salary.

In 1952 Mátyás Rákosi became Hungary's leader. His policies almost ruined the country financially, and the people were extremely discontented. The following year Imre Nagy replaced Rákosi, but Rákosi still led the Communist Party. In 1955 Hungary joined the Warsaw Pact, a political-military alliance between other Eastern European communist countries.

Nagy's policies provided improved living conditions and increased personal freedom. Rákosi opposed these reforms and in 1955 forced Nagy out of the party and the government. Rákosi's policies made things difficult for the youth of the country and any who wished to express themselves freely. Although Rákosi was replaced, his policies were not, igniting the revolution of 1956. Imre Nagy, once again in control, declared Hungary a neutral country. A few days later his government was ended when Soviet forces invaded, arresting and killing those involved in the uprising. In 1958 Nagy and his supporters were tried and executed.

Communist Control Tightens

Following the 1956 revolution, the Soviet Union controlled Hungary tightly. At first, János Kádár, leader of Hungary's Communist Party on and off from 1956, carried out policies designed to prevent another revolution. In the early 1960s Kádár's government, anxious for more support from the Hungarian people, loosened its control of all aspects of Hungarian life.

In 1968 a free market system, the New Economic Mechanism, was introduced. It was a system in which individuals, rather than the government, made economic decisions. Productivity increased and living standards improved. In the 1970s raw material costs increased and economic growth slowed, resulting in inflation and a trade deficit. Living conditions worsened. Communist Party opposition prevented the system from being completely successful, and the program ended in the early 1980s. In 1985 the Congress of the Hungarian Socialist Workers' Party ended after János Kádár was reelected as party leader.

A New Constitution Marks the End of Communism

In 1988 Kádár's opposition to further reforms caused his replacement as Communist Party leader. Under Károly Grósz, major economic changes occurred. Company managers gained

People hold flags in front of parliament on October 23, 1989, as the newly renamed Republic of Hungary holds the promise of multiparty elections and the end of communism.

increased authority. Privately owned businesses were encouraged, particularly those in partnerships with foreign companies. By 1989 new political parties began appearing, including some that had disappeared in the 1940s under communist rule. In October 1989 the Communist Party, no longer all-powerful, renamed itself the Hungarian Socialist Party. Some communist leaders opposing this change created the Hungarian Workers' Party.

It was time for a new constitution. A multiparty democratic government was formed and people again had religious freedom. A new office was created, that of president. Mátyás Szrös served as interim president until multiparty elections—the first since 1949—were held in 1990. Árpád Göncz became the new president. The noncommunist Hungarian Democratic Forum gained the most votes, and the first major changes began. Most state and collective farms were split up and the newly created small farms were sold to private owners. The remainder continued being run by businesses or the government. In 1999

Hungary joined the North Atlantic Treaty Organization (NATO), a military alliance of Western countries.

In 1994, in new elections, the Hungarian Socialist Party (mostly led by former Communists) had earned the most votes. Forming a coalition government with the Alliance of Free Democrats, the new leadership continued reforms already in progress. In the presidential elections of 1995 Göncz again became president.

In the 1998 elections a conservative third party came into power, the Federation of Young Democrats-Hungarian Civic Party. In 2000 Ferenc Mádl became president, and in the 2002 elections a coalition of Hungarian Socialists and Free Democrats were returned to power. Hungary has been a member of the United Nations since 1995, and on May 1, 2004, joined the European Union.

Hungarian president
Ferenc Mádl (center)

Hungary's Government

THE REPUBLIC OF HUNGARY HAS A SYSTEM OF GOVERN-ment known as a parliamentary democracy. For Hungary, it means a multiparty system of government where the public has the power to elect the people they want to represent them. It also means that all forms of ownership and private enterprise are available to everyone. Its laws are based on a constitution. Hungary's capital city is Budapest, and the country is administered from the Parliament House there.

Opposite: **The Hungarian flag at the Parliament House in Budapest**

In 1949 Hungary's laws were modeled after the communist constitution of the Soviet Union. Hungary remained a one-party state until 1988, although in 1972 there was some revision of its laws and structure. Until 1990 both the executive and legislative branches of the government were controlled by the only political party, the Hungarian Socialist Workers' Party (HSWP).

The Executive Branch

The executive branch is led by the president (chief of state). Since he was elected on June 6, 2000, Ferenc Mádl has served in this position. He is the commander in chief of the armed forces, authorizes elections, and serves

NATIONAL GOVERNMENT OF HUNGARY

Executive Branch

CHIEF OF STATE (PRESIDENT)

HEAD OF GOVERNMENT (PRIME MINISTER)

CABINET (COUNCIL OF MINISTERS)

Legislative Branch

NATIONAL ASSEMBLY (386 MEMBERS)

Judicial Branch

SUPREME COURT JUDGES

Hungarian prime minister Péter Medgyessy (left) meets with U.S. president George W. Bush in June 2004.

as a one-man parliament during the period between National Assembly (parliament) sessions. Presidents are elected by the National Assembly, serve for a five-year term, and may be reelected for a second term.

The head of the government is the prime minister. He is elected by the National Assembly on the recommendation of the president. Since May 2002, the prime minister has been Péter Medgyessy. The cabinet is a council of ministers elected by the National Assembly on the recommendation of the president. The cabinet serves for four years. It makes the day-to-day decisions necessary in running the country.

The Legislative Branch

The legislative branch is a unicameral, single body that consists of 386 members. The members are elected by popular vote and serve for four years. Hungary has a number of political parties. They include the Alliance of Free Democrats, the Christian Democratic People's Party, the Hungarian Civic Alliance, the Hungarian Democratic Forum, the Hungarian Democratic People's Party, the Hungarian Justice and Life Party, the Hungarian Socialist Party, and the Hungarian Workers' Party. During the elections in spring 2002 a coalition of the Hungarian Socialist Party and the Alliance of Free Democrats Party won by the smallest margin in Hungarian

Parliament in session

history, gaining only 51.19 percent of the vote. This gave them only a 10-seat majority in the 386-seat parliament. Other political parties currently represented in Hungary's parliament are the Hungarian Civic Alliance (the Alliance of Young Democrats) and the Hungarian Democratic Forum.

The Seat of Hungary's Government

On October 12, 1885, ground was broken on the Pest side of the Danube for a permanent parliament building. For forty years, contests had been held to select a designer for the building, and in 1882 a winner, Emmerich von Steindl, was selected. Plans were made to construct his design, which combined old and new style elements with modern building techniques. Since the Renaissance, architects often combined Greek and Roman styles with ornate baroque styles or the romantic concepts of the Renaissance.

Steindl felt it wasn't appropriate to create a totally new architectural style. The magnificent domed exterior of his parliament building is described as Gothic Revival, a style that developed in European and American architecture in the eighteenth and nineteenth centuries. Where sections of the interior needed to serve particular functions, he simplified his design.

Inside the building, a sweeping staircase rises from the main entrance. The statue-lined domed hall at the top of the stairs (above) creates a sensation of immense space. In the huge dining hall the frescoed walls and ceiling bear a Lake Balaton fishing scene, Hungary's castles, several allegorical figures, and scenes from Hungary's history. Among the building's magnificent spaces are reception rooms, a delegation room, council chambers, and those that host parliamentary sessions. Hungarians are truly proud of this national treasure.

The Judicial Branch

Hungarian justice is administered by a number of bodies: the Supreme Court, which is a branch of the national government and the country's highest court, the Budapest Metropolitan Court, and city, county, district, labor, and military courts. City and district courts serve in much the same way as the lower courts do in the United States. Most disputes are first dealt with at this level of the court system.

Supreme Court judges are elected by the National Assembly and serve nine-year terms. Their main responsibility is to ensure that the legislative branch adheres to the articles of the constitution. They have the final word on all important legal matters.

The Constitution

Today's constitution consists of seventy-eight articles and almost four hundred phrases. These articles and phrases are

Hungary's Flag

Hungary has had several flags throughout its history. The Austro-Hungarian flag, introduced in 1867, consisted of three horizontal bars of equal width; red upper bar, white middle, and a half red, half green, lower section. This was a blend of the red-white-red Austrian flag and the Hungarian red-white-green flag. The flag of the ruling Hapsburgs had two equal-sized horizontal stripes in yellow and black. Today's flag has the original red-white-green horizontal stripes, the traditional national colors.

the body of laws and legal procedures by which the government runs the country. Over the last fifty-plus years the constitution has gone through some major changes. In June 1948 the Hungarian Workers' Party (later renamed the Hungarian Socialist Workers' Party), began work on a constitution that recognized the changes occurring in what was still a Communist-controlled country—changes in society, economy, and daily living. Constitutional laws were modeled after the Soviet Union's 1936 Stalin constitution.

In 1972, as things began to change in Hungary and communism became less powerful, the constitution was again reviewed and some changes were made. In the 1949 constitution, for example, the only group entitled to full civil rights were named as "workers." In 1972 the term was changed to "citizens." Then, in spring 1988, the National Assembly approved amendments to the constitution. Most important, it allowed for a multiparty system. The one-party state was replaced by a representative democracy. Approximately one hundred constitutional changes were made in the creation of the new system. The dominant party, the HSWP, changed its name to the Hungarian Socialist Party, one of a number of parties vying for leadership in the government.

Hungary's national minorities recently gained both attention and importance. Among some recent constitutional articles is a guarantee of equal rights and the free use of their mother tongue to all national minorities. In 1990 an Office of National and Ethnic Minorities was established in order to protect the rights of those minority groups.

Lajos Kossuth: Revolutionary and Leader

Lajos Kossuth, an attorney, lived from 1802 to 1894. Constantly in trouble with the government for his radical views, he was imprisoned in 1836 for publishing material critical of the government. In 1848 Kossuth demanded an independent government for Hungary, and when the Austrian Hapsburgs and Hungary went to war later that year, he became provisional governor of Hungary.

The following year Kossuth named himself president and declared Hungary's independence, but he refused to grant independence to minority groups. Although Hungary successfully pushed back the Austrian army, Kossuth's regime ended soon when the Russian czarist armies joined the battle. The year 1849 brought the end of the fighting as well as a compromise—the creation of the Austro-Hungarian Empire, which gave Hungary some autonomy. Kossuth's vision of a Hungary with a democratic system and parliamentary representation was not to be.

To escape death, Kossuth fled first to Turkey, where he was held prisoner for a time, then to the United States. There he joined a group of refugees who had established the community of New Buda in Iowa. He made speeches all over the United States and even made a powerful speech in the U.S. Congress on the subject of democracy. Although he never gave up trying, he was unable to return to power in Hungary.

During the communist years, Hungary's Communist Youth League (Kommunista Ifúsági Szövetség—KISZ) was the official youth organization of Hungary. Sponsored by the HSWP, Hungary's only political party at the time, the organization was open to young people ages fourteen to twenty-six. Many members, however, were over the age limit.

In the 1980s about 800,000 young people belonged to the Communist Youth League. Among university students, 96 percent were members. Of those young people who were part of Hungary's workforce, 31 percent were members. The

Young Pioneers perform at Hungary's largest Pioneer camp, Zanka, in 1973.

Hungary's National Anthems

The words of the national anthem sung in Hungary today are very different from those sung when Hungary was under the control of the Austrian Hapsburgs:

God preserve, God bless,
Our Emperor, our country!
Powerful through faith's support
May he lead us with a wise hand!
His father's crown let us
Shield against every enemy!
Austria's fortune stays reconciled!

The current anthem was written by Ferenc Kölcsey (1790–1838) with music by Ferenc Erkel (1810–1893).

God bless the Hungarians
With good cheer and prosperity.
Extend a protective arm
If they fight the enemy.
Torn by misfortune for long,
Give them happy years.
These people have expiated
The past and the future.

organization sought to represent the country's youth, educate them politically, and provide social activities. Young people were encouraged to be politically active, but they also lent a hand in factories or helped farmers at harvesttime.

During those same communist years, a separate organization, the Association of Young Pioneers, was formed for children aged six to fourteen. Most young people became members; meetings took place in school classrooms, and the groups' leaders tried to teach the children about Marxist/Leninist ideals. Groups of Young Pioneers, in their red ties and white shirts, were a common sight on special occasions and at summer camps that were organized for them.

April 1989 marked the end of these two strong youth organizations. Communism was over and it was time for a change. The Democratic Youth Federation is a voluntary league of youth organizations, none of which can accept direction or input from any political party.

Budapest: Did You Know This?

Excavations have revealed that both Bronze and Iron Age people lived in the area. Celts and Romans also had settlements there, but it didn't become Budapest until 1873 when Pest, Buda, and Obuda (Old Buda) became one city. Today's city lies on both banks of the Danube River. The two halves are connected by seven road bridges and two railway bridges. Of its twenty-three districts, sixteen are on the Pest side and six are in Buda. Budapest is nicknamed the "town of baths."

Budapest is one of the loveliest of all European capitals. Buda's Castle Hill, on the western side of the river, was named a World Heritage Site in 1987. Gellért Hill

and the Castle District (below) are shaded with many huge old trees. Cobbled streets and such spectacular medieval buildings as the Royal Palace and Mátyás Church please the eye. Some buildings are pastel-colored. From the Fisherman's Bastion one sees breathtaking views of the entire city. Below the hill on the Pest side of the river is the massive Parliament House. At night, looking across the river from mostly flat, crowded Pest, the illuminated Castle Hill in Buda is a wondrous sight.

Population: 2 million

Year founded: 1873, three towns merged, becoming one.

Average daily temperature in January: 32°F (0°C)

Average daily temperature in July: 71°F (21.6°C)

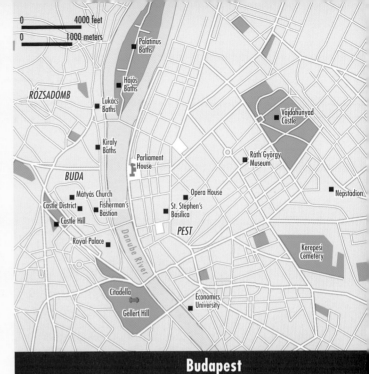

Budapest

Farming, Mining, and Industry

BEFORE THE OUTBREAK OF WORLD WAR II IN 1939, MOST Hungarian farms belonged to the nobility. They employed large numbers of farmhands. At that time, half of Hungary's population was involved in farming. Farm laborers had only small areas of land for themselves, on which they grew fruit trees and enough vegetables for their own consumption. Geese and chickens in front and back yards or wandering down rural streets were a common sight.

During Hungary's communist-ruled postwar years, 94 percent of farmland was owned by cooperatives or the state. Farm laborers (peasants) worked hard and earned little. Today, farms are once again privately owned. Although only 6.2 percent of the population is now involved in farming, Hungary continues to produce most of the food it consumes and even exports fruit, vegetables, and meat.

Since World War II, considerable industrialization has occurred throughout the country. Many people now work in factories instead of on farms. Gradually, Hungary has changed from having a socialized economy to a free market economy. Some of the many new businesses that have sprung up are joint ventures with foreign investors.

Opposite: **A woman stacks bundles of hay between rows of corn on a Hungarian farm.**

Crops

Hungarian farmers have two great assets: rich soil and a climate that is favorable for crop production. Variations in the

Irrigation ensures a hearty crop of corn for this farm.

weather, however, cause productivity to vary from year to year. Since eastern Hungary is drier than the west, droughts sometimes occur. Rain, extreme heat, and severe frosts are also dangerous to crops.

Irrigation systems have become vital to the success of each harvest. More and more irrigation channels are being used to deliver water from the Tisza and Danube rivers to wherever it is needed. Pipes and spray irrigation are used for farms farthest from the rivers.

Common crops are barley, wheat, and sweet corn. Using modern equipment, harvesting begins in the summer months, ending with the gathering of corn in October. Not only do the barley, wheat, and corn grains become flour, the stems provide food for cattle and sheep during the winter months. Potatoes, rice, and tobacco also are common crops.

Hungary's Currency

Hungary's money is based on the decimal system. Items are paid for using a monetary unit called a forint. Forint notes are issued in denominations of Ft 200, 500, 1,000, 2,000, 5,000, 10,000, 20,000. Forint coins come in denominations of 1, 2, 5, 10, 20, 50, 100, and 200, although Ft 200 coins are rare. In international business and banking circles, forints are often referred to as HUF. In October 2004 U.S.$1=200.02 forints (Ft).

Each of Hungary's seven forint notes (below) pictures someone significant in Hungary's history on one side. An illustration of a place or event associated with the person is shown on the back. For instance, on the front of the green 200 Ft note is the fourteenth-century king, Charles Robert, and his castle at Diósgyör near Miskolc on the back. The blue 1,000 Ft note has the portrait of King Matthias Corvinus on one side, with Hercules's

Well at Visegrád Castle on the reverse. The purple 5,000 Ft note has Count István Széchenyi, sometimes referred to as the Greatest Hungarian, on the front, with his family home at Nagycenk on the back.

Now that Hungary has joined the European Union it is expected that within two years Hungary will adopt the euro (above) as its monetary unit. In April 2003 Hungarians voted overwhelmingly in favor of the euro.

Sugar beets, grown in Hungary's northwest, are one of Hungary's most profitable crops. The sugar is extracted in factories, and the remaining pulp is returned to the farmer. Along with beet leaves, the pulp provides yet another source of cattle food. Once harvested by hand, the beets are now topped and then taken from the soil by machine.

Farmers also grow large numbers of gherkins, a small type of cucumber. Pickled in a vinegar-water mix flavored with spices, salt, and sugar, gherkins are exported all over Europe. Since Hungarians enjoy spicy foods, herbs of various kinds are also common crops. Red clover is raised for feeding horses and cattle.

Flowers and Fruits

Six-foot-tall sunflowers are grown for their seeds. The seeds yield oil that is used in salads, for cooking, and in margarine

Sunflowers produce seeds and oil that contribute to Hungary's economy.

Help is welcome from all during the fall harvest of wine grapes.

production. Poppies, another colorful, common sight, are also cultivated for their seeds. The seeds are dried for use in cake fillings or sprinkled on breads and pastries.

Hungary's orchards produce mulberries, apples, pears, cherries, and apricots. These are sold fresh or dried. Most apricots are grown for jam in orchards south of Lake Balaton. Overripe fruit, such as apricots, goes to distilleries. There it ferments in vats, using much the same method by which grapes are made into wines. The result is one of Hungary's favorite drinks, apricot brandy.

A number of Hungarian regions are blessed with sunny slopes and rich soil, perfect locations for growing grapes. From June onward, caring for the vines is a full-time job, as they are pruned and sprayed to protect them against bugs, mildew, or diseases. The autumn grape picking is a festive time. Local people, young and old, help with the harvest and join the farmers in celebrating a successful harvest.

Hungarian Cowboys

Csikós, Hungarian cowboys, are a common sight on large collective farms where herds of horses and cattle roam the puszta. When rounding up the animals for branding, they carry long whips and lassos and wear high boots with spurs. To contact each other, the cowboys make sharp sounds on a cow horn.

The csikós celebrate their hard day's work with hearty stews, coarse white bread, and beer or apricot brandy. Often music and folk songs complete the celebration. On some occasions the csikós still dress in traditional clothing—a small-brimmed black hat and perhaps a long white cloak. Others wear black vests, the same style of hat, natural-colored wide-sleeved shirts, and wide-legged trousers.

Livestock

Hungary has numerous sheep and once had large herds of cattle. Since 1990, the government has enforced a reduction in the numbers of livestock in order to combat overpopulation. As has happened for centuries, each spring, cattle are driven out onto the plains. Herdsmen accompany them, live in tiny wooden huts, then herd the animals back to farm pens in the fall. Dairy products and meat are two of Hungary's important industries. Leather goods are manufactured from cattle hides.

Hungary has always had large numbers of horses, many for pulling farm carts or equipment. Hungary is famous for its spirited Lipizzaner. Usually gray and smooth-coated, these horses

The Lippizzaner

are intelligent, gentle, and good workers. They usually become white-coated as they age, similar to the famous Austrian performing horses. Shagya Arabian horses were originally imported from Arabia. The large Hungarian-bred Furioso is well suited for equestrian sports like racing and jumping. Also Hungarian-bred, the heavy Nonius is a workhorse.

Manufacturing, Mining, and Service Industries

After World War II, Hungary found itself in ruins. Factories, bridges, and railways were rebuilt first. Through a series of five-year plans, transportation systems improved. As heavy and light industries started up, the nation rapidly became industrialized.

Hungary's main products are railroad and transportation equipment, textiles, foods, beverages, chemicals, pharmaceuticals, plastics, steel, aluminum, and machinery. Although most factories are in the Budapest area, the island of Csepel, located between the two branches of the Danube River south of Budapest, is home to engineering companies, factories producing steel, iron, electronic equipment, paper, leather, and fur goods. Its riverfront port handles international river traffic. Debrecen, Hungary's second largest city, is a center for trade and handicrafts. Miskolc, Hungary's third largest city,

Weights and Measures

Hungary uses the metric system of measurement. Distance is measured in centimeters, meters, and kilometers instead of inches, yards, and miles.

10 millimeters (mm) = 1 centimeter (cm)

100 centimeters = 1 meter (m)

1 meter = 39.37 inches (in)

1 kilometer (km) = 0.621 miles

Liquid is measured in milliliters and liters instead of cups, pints, quarts, and gallons.

1,000 ml = 1 liter (l)

1 liter = 1.057 quarts (qt)

Metric weights are measured in grams and kilograms.

1,000 grams (g) = 1 kilogram (kg)

1 kilogram = 2.205 pounds (lb)

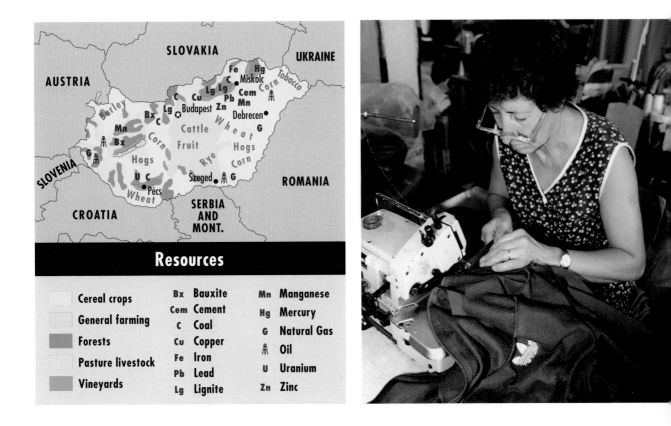

Resources

☐ Cereal crops	Bx	Bauxite	Mn	Manganese
☐ General farming	Cem	Cement	Hg	Mercury
☐ Forests	C	Coal	G	Natural Gas
☐ Pasture livestock	Cu	Copper	⚒	Oil
☐ Vineyards	Fe	Iron	U	Uranium
	Pb	Lead	Zn	Zinc
	Lg	Lignite		

produces furniture, food products, glass, textiles, and cement. Pécs is a center for fruit (including grapes), vegetables, tobacco, and coal mining.

Even though much of the population still has a poor standard of living, Hungary is Central Europe's most economically developed country. On May 1, 2004, Hungary became a member of the European Union, endorsed by most citizens. The gross domestic product is climbing rapidly as increasing numbers of people buy cars and household appliances.

Hungary depends heavily on international trade, importing machinery, automobiles, chemicals, fertilizers, iron ore,

Textile manufacturing is a main industry in Hungary.

This port houses many containers that hold products for importing and exporting.

coal, oil, electricity, natural gas, paper, and petroleum. It exports meat, fruit and vegetables, wine, electrical equipment, steel, and transportation equipment (mainly buses and car parts).

About 59.6 percent of Hungary's workforce is employed in such service industries as education, health care, and finance (banks and the stock exchange), trades, and engineering. The engineering field and various trades employ the majority of workers.

Hungary's mineral resources are limited. Uranium is mined in the Mecsek Mountains, but since it is used in producing atomic bombs, its distribution is strictly controlled. Uranium can also be used at atomic power stations. Bauxite, used in aluminum production, is another valuable resource. In fact, 10 to 12 percent of the world's bauxite is found in Hungary's southern mountain slopes. Oil fields exist at Zala in southern Hungary, and although coal is mined in the south, the amount is insufficient for Hungary's needs. Hungary needs to continue importing coal, oil, and electricity in order for the country to fully develop.

What Hungary Grows, Makes, and Mines

Agriculture

Maize (corn)	7,857 metric tons
Wheat	5,196 metric tons
Sugar beets	2,903 metric tons

Manufacturing

Electric power	36,968 million kWh
Leather footwear	12,639,000 pairs
Cement	2,980 metric tons

Mining

Lignite	7,696 metric tons
Brown coal	6,110 metric tons
Natural gas	3,693 million cu meters

Women in the Workforce

Communism first pushed Hungarian women into the workforce. However, according to the World Bank, between 1985 and 1997 the female workforce was reduced by one-third. Since then, there has been a sudden reversal, and the female employment rate is now growing rapidly. In 2001 female unemployment was 5.1 percent, whereas male unemployment was 6.3 percent. Increasing numbers of women have entered the business world, and two out of five businesses established since 1990 are owned by women; many other women hold managerial positions in all kinds of industry.

Although discrimination exists due to the costs involved in hiring women who may need maternity and child-care benefits, there are moves toward lessening this situation. Wage discrimination also exists. According to a January 2004 source, World Bank research states that in Hungary, although salaries for women are catching up with average EU salaries, women earn only about 78 percent of what men earn, they say, owing to the "concentration of female jobs at the bottom level of the labor market." The bottom level includes such jobs as store clerks and factory workers.

The number of women in the workforce is growing in Hungary. Here a woman checks bottles at a Coca-Cola plant.

Commuters board one of Hungary's many public buses.

For single mothers, financial survival is difficult. Child care is no longer free. Many men, unhappy that women no longer are homemakers, resent their presence in the workforce. Where families can afford it, women are beginning to leave marginal jobs to stay at home.

Transportation

An efficient transportation system is vital to Hungary's industries, since large quantities of freight are transported daily. In spite of a large network of railway routes, most of today's freight travels by road. Most roads have asphalt or concrete surfaces and several international highways cross the country.

Although the network of canals and sections of the Tisza River are navigable, the Danube River is the only waterway

Cost of Meals

When you eat out in Hungary, there is a wide variety of food to choose from, particularly if you are in Buda or Pest. Not only are there restaurants specializing in Hungarian dishes but there are also French, Italian, Greek, kosher, vegetarian, Asian, and Middle Eastern restaurants. The first foreign fast food restaurant opened in 1988—a McDonalds. Burger King, Pizza Hut, and other American fast food restaurants and chain stores have opened since then.

A two-course restaurant meal with beer or wine can cost from 2000 Ft per person (U.S.$9.48) to Ft 7,000 (U.S.$33.18). Something like pizza could cost from Ft 380 (U.S.$1.80) to Ft 980 (U.S.$4.64) for one person. If you want to eat cheaply, it's best to try snacks at a sidewalk stand. Savory pancakes are Ft148 to Ft 248 (U.S.$0.70 to U.S.$1.18). Sweet pancakes cost Ft 80 to Ft 250 (U.S.$0.38 to U.S.$1.18).

Another inexpensive Hungarian snack food specialty is fözelék, which ranges in cost from 180 Ft to 260 Ft (U.S.$0.85 to U.S.$1.23). It consists of fried or boiled vegetables mixed into a white sauce made of roux (flour and fat) with sour cream.

Prices of Common Items:

McDonalds Big Mac, Ft 500 (U.S.$ 2.37)
Large French fries, Ft 330 (U.S.$1.56)
Loaf of bread, Ft 136 (U.S.$0.64)
Liter of milk, Ft 130–268 Forint (U.S.$0.62–$1.27)
1 dozen eggs, Ft 216 (U.S.$ 1.02)
Student movie ticket 470 Ft–520 (U.S.$2.23–U.S.$2.46);
adult movie ticket, Ft 980–1300 (U.S.$ 4.64–$6.16)

used for transporting goods bound for international markets. There are no internal air routes, but Malév, the national airline, flies to the Middle East and most European countries. Even so, in order to keep up with other areas of Hungary's progress, airports, railways, and roads all need to be expanded and upgraded.

An efficient public transportation system is also important to Hungary's population. Although the number of car owners is increasing, frequent buses, trolleys, and trains are absolutely necessary within cities and towns and as a link between them.

Even tiny villages are accessible by bus. Budapest's subway system, dating from 1896, is the oldest in Europe.

Tourism

As Hungary's transportation system has grown, so has the tourist industry. Although most tourists come from neighboring countries, an increasing number travel from farther afield. Castles are being renovated for new lives as resorts. Hotels and campsites are springing up everywhere, and tour companies offer an increasing number of routes. Besides visiting the country's most historic and beautiful sites and fascinating museums, visitors enjoy spas, horseback riding, hunting, or hiking.

Tourists visit Fishermen's Bastion in Budapest.

The Magyars, Minorities, and Gypsies

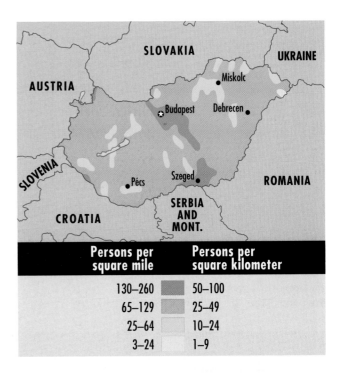

H UNGARIANS HAVE VERY FEW cultural, racial, or linguistic links with their neighbors and consider themselves to be an isolated nation. They are also a divided nation, since almost a third of Hungarians live in neighboring countries. Under the 1920 Treaty of Trianon, forced on them by the Allies after World War I (1914–1918), two-thirds of their country was parcelled out to Romania, Yugoslavia, Austria, and Czechoslovakia. Borders have changed very little since then. The Hungarian language is not related to any of the languages spoken around Hungary. It belongs to the group of Finno-Ugric languages that includes Finnish and Estonian.

The Magyars

Hungarians like to call themselves Magyars after their ancestors who settled the area twelve centuries ago. Although the Magyars aren't related to any of their near neighbors, they are related to the Finns who live far to the north of them. Migration and invasions separated the two groups over many centuries. Only a small segment of Hungary's population today is not of Magyar ancestry. These are the peoples who are

Population of Major Cities (2001 est.)

City	Population
Budapest	1,812,000
Debrecen	211,038
Miskolc	184,129
Szeged	168,276
Pécs	162,502
Gyor	129,415
Nyiregyháza	118,799
Kecskemét	107,752
Székesfehérvár	106,350

Opposite: **Hungary's population is made up of various ethnic groups.**

referred to as ethnic minorities: Romanian, Roma (Gypsy), Slovak, Serb, and German.

Another important minority group is the Jews. In spite of Hitler's persecution and murder of 6 million European Jews during World War II, a great many Hungarian Jews did sur-vive—in fact, more survived than in any other Eastern European country. Since it was not uncommon for Jews to hold prominent positions in the postwar communist government, many Hungarians associated Jews with communism; other Jews were extremely vocal in opposing communism. Today, Hungarian Jews hold responsible positions in a variety of fields of employment and are a valuable sector of the population.

Though Jews suffered during World War II in Hungary, they now are an active and important sector of the population.

Once a rural society, most Hungarians lived and worked in small communities or on the land. A lot has changed since then, as industrialization advanced. People have moved away from the countryside and now over half of the population works in industry. Twenty percent of the population live in Budapest, while 42 percent live in other large cities and towns.

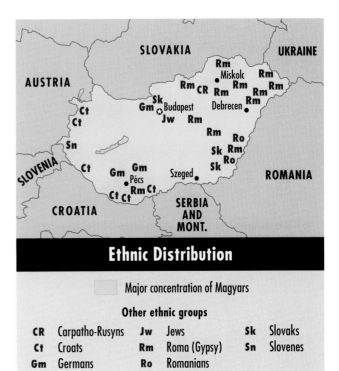

Ethnic Distribution

Major concentration of Magyars

Other ethnic groups

CR	Carpatho-Rusyns	Jw	Jews	Sk	Slovaks
Ct	Croats	Rm	Roma (Gypsy)	Sn	Slovenes
Gm	Germans	Ro	Romanians		

Hungarian Gypsies

Hungarian Gypsies, "Romanies," are a nomadic people. They have lived in Hungary for centuries and are recognized by their dark skins, darker than those of other European Gypsies. Comprising around 5 percent of Hungary's population, they live separate lives from the Magyars. Today's Gypsies are found mainly in Hungary, Romania, Bulgaria, and the region that used to be Yugoslavia.

When their wandering ancestors left India in A.D. 1000, Gypsies gradually moved west, settling in Central Europe in the 1400s. At first their presence was welcomed mainly for their skill as ironworkers. In Hungary, though, Magyar rulers treated them as slaves, even selling them at slave markets.

During World War II, Hitler's Nazis rounded up Gypsies and others considered "racially impure." Many Gypsies were

Ethnic Breakdown

Gypsies (Romanies)	142,683
Germans	37,511
Croats	17,577
Slovaks	12,745
Poles	10,000
Romanians	8,730
Russians	6,000
Bulgarians	3,000
Greeks	3,000
Serbs	2,953
Slovenes	2,627
Ukrainians	2,000
Armenians	1,500

In Hungary, the Gypsy
community is recognized as
an ethnic minority.

murdered in concentration camps. During communism,
Gypsies were blamed for not contributing to the socialist system. Today, the prejudice shown toward them is reappearing.
They are often blamed for everything from crime to unemployment. Through it all, though, they have hung on fiercely
to their Romany accent and ancient customs.

Some Gypsies are known worldwide for their colorful costumes and the vigorous music that has been handed down from father to son for centuries. Orchestras usually consist of a bass, clarinet, two fiddles, and a cimbalom, an instrument similar to a large dulcimer and played with two small hammers. Today it is common for Hungarian restaurants to feature Gypsy musicians. In past centuries Gypsies entertained at royal courts and military events, and even provided the stirring music that sent troops into battle.

Gypsies have held on to their culture through dance, as well as music.

Common Words and Phrases

Jó napot kívánok.	Hello.
Jó reggelt.	Good morning.
Jó estét.	Good evening.
Köszönöm.	Thank you.
Hogy van?	How are you?
Hogy hívjak?	What's your name?
A nevem . . .	My name is . . .
Akarok menni . . .	I want to go to . . .
Mennyibe kerül?	How much is it?
Hol van . . . ?	Where is . . . ?

Family ties are strong in Hungary.

Today's Hungarians

Hungarians are creative, ambitious, serious, and extremely polite people. Even when greeting a good friend they shake hands. On a visit to someone's home, it is important to present the hostess with flowers or a bottle of wine. Everything is an acceptable subject for conversation—except money. Talking about how much one earns is considered inappropriate and rude.

In cities and towns, an average family has only one or two children and it is common for both parents to work full-time. In rural areas, a family might have three children. Gypsy families often have three or more children. Family connections are important, and relatives get together for family celebrations whenever possible. Families freely help each other out in any way possible. Parental discipline is strict, and in preparation for working hard as adults, children are taught to help around the house or in the family vegetable garden. In farming families, the children work in the fields.

In many ways, Hungary was the most relaxed of the communist countries. Their standard of living was higher than their neighbors'. To achieve that higher standard and buy even the most basic necessities, most men worked two or three jobs and their wives also worked full-time. Very young children spent many hours in some type of child care.

Health care was free under communism. Since 1992, workers must contribute at least 10 percent of their income to medical insurance. Private medical care is also available.

The Hungarian Language

Hungarian is not an easy language to learn, and with its many accent marks it is also difficult to read and write. Nevertheless, the pronunciation of vowel and consonant sounds rarely changes no matter where the letters are used.

Pronunciation Key

Vowels:

a - like the *o* in dot

á - like the *a* in rather

e - like the *e* in get

é - like the *a* in say (without the y sound)

i - a little like the *i* in sit

í - like the *ee* in fleece

o - like the *o* in over

ó - a longer version of the o above

ö - as the *o* in word (without the r sound)

ő - a longer version of the ö

u - like the *u* in push

ú - like the *oo* in mood

ü - similar to the *u* in cute

ű - a more breathy, longer version of the ü

Consonants:

c - like the *ts* in cats

cs - like the *ch* in chocolate

gy - like the *j* in jewelry but with the tongue pressed against the roof of the mouth

j - like the *y* in yellow

ly - the sound of *y* in yes but with a slight *l* sound

ny - like the *ni* in dominion

r - trilled like the *r* in many Scottish words

s - like the *sh* as in sharp

sz - like the *s* in sad

ty - like the *tu* in tune

w - like the *v* in van

zs - like the *s* in measure

It is important for employees of Hungarian businesses to speak multiple languages.

If Hungarians want to communicate with their European neighbors, it is essential that they learn the languages that will be most useful to them in the business world. During the communist period, Russian was taught in primary and secondary schools. Today it is more common for schoolchildren and adults to study English, German, and other languages.

Modern Hungarian is the result of a variety of influences. It was originally a Magyar tribal language. As different invaders took control of Hungary, the language gradually began to change. Over the centuries the Turks and Slavs left their trace in the language. Later, French and Latin were added to the mix.

Since sentences often start right out with whatever the speaker wants to emphasize, they are spoken in mixed-up order. You can tell whether a noun is a subject or object by its

Forms of Address

Prior to communism each person was addressed in a way that indicated his or her ranking in society. There were social levels even among farm workers. The horsemen, *csikosok*, ranked at the top; with cowherds, *gulyasok*, next; then *pasztorok*, shepherds. Swineherds, *kanaszok*, were at the bottom of the social ladder. During communism, everyone became *elvtárs*, comrades. Today adults are addressed with the formal *ön* unless they indicate that the informal *te* is acceptable. Married people use *ön* when addressing their in-laws. Using correct greetings is important.

When writing or telling their names, Hungarians always put their last name first, a custom normally associated with Asian cultures. Their title, Mr. or Mrs., for example, follows. In Hungarian Mr. John Smith would be Kovács János úr (Smith John Mr.).

suffix. There are also no male or female nouns, as in French and Spanish, but the suffix né is added if the person being named by the noun is female.

Hungarian has been "standardized." Although in some small villages an older form of Hungarian may still be spoken, the standardized language has no major dialects and varies little from region to region. In the nineteenth century, through an effort by politicians and poets, Hungarian (Magyar) became everyone's primary language. In some regions, however, where large numbers of such minorities as Romanians or Germans are living, street signs or signs on stores might be in the other language, too. Most Gypsies also speak Hungarian, but some speak only Romany. Since the Gypsies originated in India, their language, Romany, is based on ancient Sanskrit.

Even though the Hungarian language has been standardized, those in rural regions still speak an older version of the language.

Religion in Hungary

Close to two-thirds of Hungary's people are Roman Catholic, and have been since King Stephen I was crowned in the year 1000. He and his wife, Gisela, worked tirelessly to convert the people to Christianity, and in 1083 he was made a saint in recognition of this work. Saint Stephen has been the much-loved patron saint of Hungary ever since.

When the Communists gained control in the late 1940s, religion was discouraged but not forbidden. In the 1960s Communist opposition to religion became less strict, and Hungarians resumed attending churches and synagogues in large numbers.

Religion Through the Centuries

When the Magyars arrived in Hungary, they brought with them their pagan beliefs. However, King Stephen realized that in order for Hungary to survive in Europe and develop a national identity, conversion to Christianity was an important step. His father, Duke Geza, had already chosen Rome over Byzantium by selecting Western Christianity (Roman Catholicism) over the Eastern Orthodox Church after being defeated by the Germans in 955. Hungary had allied with Rome for protection. In only a few years, the country had been converted to Christianity.

From 1569 to 1699 the Turks ruled central and southern Hungary. The Hapsburg kingdom ruled the north, and in the east, princes ruled the principality of Transylvania. Being a

Opposite: **Roman Catholicism is practiced by more than half of all Hungarians.**

Founder of the Hungarian Catholic Religion

Stephen (István) was born in Esztergom in 975. At age ten he and his father were baptized as Catholics. After a defeat at the hands of Germany, it had become politically necessary for Hungary's elite to become Catholics if they were to become integrated into the rest of Europe. At age twenty, Stephen married Gisela. Two years later he succeeded his father as Duke of Hungary. After waging war in uniting the country, Stephen gained control by reducing the power of the nobles, abolishing tribal divisions, and establishing counties administered by governors. Stephen then sent an emissary, Anastasius (Saint Astrius), to Rome to ask Pope Sylvester II to anoint him king.

In A.D. 1000, Stephen, wearing the crown sent to him by Pope Sylvester, became Hungary's first king. He established churches and monasteries and made Christianity the state religion. Anyone found practicing paganism, with its superstitions and beliefs, was dealt with severely. With the exception of the clergy, everyone was ordered to marry, but marriage between pagans and Christians was forbidden. Tithes were collected to support the poor, and every tenth town was required to have a church. King Stephen was accessible to everyone and was a great supporter of the poor. Hungary's patron saint's image is seen throughout the country.

Christian country, Hungary participated in the religious crusades that were mounted against the Turks.

In the sixteenth century Protestant movements against the Roman Catholic Church (a period known as the Reformation) spread across Europe to Hungary. Those who had fought for Hungarian independence against the Hapsburgs were mostly Protestants. In 1699, when the Hapsburgs were victorious over the Turks, Hungary became part of the Austrian Hapsburg Empire with the Hapsburgs established as Hungary's sole rulers. Those who fought for independence during a Catholic counterrevolutionary movement that occurred throughout Europe were punished by the Hapsburgs, who for two hundred years ruled Hungary as a primarily Catholic country.

The Crown of Saint Stephen

One of the most spectacular artifacts that might be seen in any museum is the Crown of Saint Stephen. Housed in Parliament House, it is displayed along with a ceremonial sword, an orb, and a tenth-century crystal-headed scepter. According to legend, around the year 1000, Asztrik, the first abbot of the Pannonhalma monastery in Western Transdanubia, presented the crown to Stephen. It legitimized Stephen's rule as the new king and assured his loyalty to Rome and the Catholic Church. Over the centuries, the crown has disappeared several times. At one point it was dropped and has been crooked ever since.

In 1945 fascists fleeing the Russians took the crown to Austria. From there it was taken to Kentucky's Fort Knox. It was returned to Hungary in 1978 by President Jimmy Carter. The crown is extremely important to the Hungarian people. Whenever justice is dispensed, it is always done "in the name of Saint Stephen's Crown." On January 1, 2000, to mark its millennium, it was moved with great ceremony from the Hungarian National Museum in Budapest to Parliament House.

Hungary's Jews

Hungary's Jews originated in three different areas of Europe and Asia. Those who arrived first came as servants of the Magyar tribes who settled the area. Others came from southeastern Poland, while a third group fled from the persecution inflicted upon them in Spain. The most Orthodox of them lived apart from the rest of the Jews, and governed themselves with severe religious laws. In time, many Jews held responsible governmental and professional positions and were highly regarded as businessmen.

Before World War II, the Jewish population was ten times the size it is today. The Holocaust eliminated most Jewish

Hungarians gather at the Great Synagogue to remember the victims of World War II.

The Great Synagogue

Not only is the Great Synagogue important to the Budapest Jewish community, it is considered one of the world's most unique architectural masterpieces. Able to seat up to 3,000 people, it is the largest synagogue in Europe and the second largest in the world. During such important celebrations as Yom Kippur, an equal number of people are often outside listening to the service.

Completed in 1859, the synagogue's architecture was inspired by the Great Synagogue of Vienna which, along with many of Europe's other synagogues, was burned down by Hitler's troops. Designed by Austrian architect Ludwig Förster, two onion-domed towers reach into the sky high above the rest of the building; the many arches of the interior were decorated with colorful Oriental, Byzantine, and Mesopotamian motifs.

World-famous composers Franz Liszt and Camille Saint-Saëns have played the synagogue's organ, and famous rabbis have led services there. During World War II the synagogue was a place of refuge for Jews forced to live in ghettos and work for the Germans. During the siege of Budapest in 1945, the synagogue was hit seventeen times. Renovation began in 1991 and continues to this day.

communities. Well over 500,000 Hungarian Jews were killed by the Nazis. Many were deported to Nazi concentration camps and died there. In 1956, eleven years after the war, a great many Jews emigrated to the United States, Palestine (the state of Israel), or to other parts of the world accepting them. Hungary's Jews today number about 100,000. Most of them take pride in thinking of themselves first as Hungarian as well as Jewish.

Communist Atheism

Atheists believe that there is no God. The ideals of communism were totally opposite to the beliefs of Hungary's Christians. Christianity promises that judgment for sins will occur in heaven. Communism asserts that justice should be administered on earth.

Under communism, there could be only one system of leadership. The church—and God—must no longer be all-powerful. To achieve this, the Communists harassed priests, damaged churches, and took away the land owned by the Catholic Church. In 1948 Cardinal József Mindszenty, Hungary's highest Catholic official, was imprisoned.

Religious Calendar

Lent	Forty days prior to Easter
Good Friday and Easter Sunday	March or April
Whitsunday (Pentecost)	May or June
Feast of Saint Stephen	August 20
All Saints Day	November 1
Visit by Saint Nicholas	December 6
Christmas Day	December 25

Communism and Religion

In 1945, as World War II ended and before the Communists took over as the supreme power, the Catholic Church lost the

Matthias Church

The Church of Our Lady (Nagyboldogasszony Templom) is usually known as Matthias Church. King Matthias (Mátyás) was the most popular of the Hungarian kings.

Located in the Castle district of Buda, Matthias Church overlooks the Square of the Holy Trinity. It is a symbol of Buda and a popular tourist attraction. Sections of the church were built in the thirteenth century, but the central part of the church was constructed around 1400. During Turkish rule, the furnishings were removed, the interior walls whitewashed and decorated with inscriptions from the Koran. Later it was converted into a baroque Catholic church.

During the siege of Budapest in 1945, the structure was badly damaged but has since been restored to its original style. It has high vaulted ceilings and Gothic pillars.

ownership of all its property in the first of the land reforms. Three years later, most religious orders were disbanded, Catholic clubs were terminated, and religious schools were taken over by the state. In 1950 one-fourth of Hungary's monks and nuns were deported, and religious publications were banned.

Since all of these upheavals meant that religious ceremonies throughout the Eastern European countries had been banned, the Communists developed their own versions of baptism, communion, weddings, and funerals. They became state ceremonies. However, in Hungary the new forms of ceremonies were not enforced, and people continued to hold church ceremonies for events such as weddings.

In exchange for being allowed to do this, the churches reached an agreement with the communist government. They accepted the Communist Party as the supreme authority. They would follow its rules. Hungarians had never been overly religious, so the arrangement suited everyone. Church attendance was low before the arrival of communism and it continued to be low.

Unlike Catholics, Protestants accepted the Communist takeover and by the late 1940s had reached agreements with them. As a result, they had more freedom than Catholics and retained the right to worship. Many Protestants even supported communist doctrines and some felt they had reached a point where all religions would be treated equally. Some even became active followers of the revolution of 1956.

By 1964 things had improved. The state (the Communist Party) reached an agreement with the Vatican. Church officials took an oath of allegiance to the Hungarian constitution and the country's laws and accepted the state's right to approve the selection of important church officials. Gradually church posts were filled, and the church was able to revive traditional ceremonies.

Major Religions (2002 Census)	
Roman Catholic	67.5%
Calvinist	20%
Jewish, other, and no religion	7.5%
Lutheran	5%

In 1974 relationships between the Catholic Church and communist leaders improved even more when the Vatican officially removed Cardinal Mindszenty from office. He was allowed to leave Hungary. In order to protect himself from the Communists, he had been living safely in the American embassy in Budapest for many years.

Religion Today

In the 1980s, when communist influence lessened, church attendance among Roman Catholics increased. However, the number of clergymen decreased (mainly because a great many had reached retirement age), and the Church had difficulty staffing their many churches. A big step forward occurred in 1989 when the government abolished the State Office for Church Affairs. In its place the government planned to establish a National Church Council. The council would act as consultants for, not as controllers of, church-related matters. Church affairs became the responsibility of the Ministry of Culture.

The Cross and the Crown: Hungary's Coat of Arms

In 1990, when a new parliament was elected, one of the first items on their agenda was the question of whether or not to bring back Hungary's traditional coat of arms. Known as a *címer*, the coat of arms was once an important national symbol. It had first appeared during the 1848 Revolution when Lajos Kossuth led the country.

The coat of arms, shaped like a shield, has the crown of Saint Stephen at the top and a double-barred cross on the right. Although over half of Hungary's population are Roman Catholics, many parliamentarians felt that the Christian symbols interfered with the principal of separation of church and state. Some members of parliament felt that the coat-of-arms was acceptable to them if the cross was removed. However, when it came to a vote, the cross stayed. The coat of arms was accepted just as it was.

Gradually an increasing number of Christian churches have been either repaired or built, the Jewish community constructed a new synagogue, religious publications appeared once again, and religious services are sometimes broadcast. A few church-affiliated colleges now exist.

Every few years census takers note an increase in the number of people attending churches and synagogues. The main religion is still Christianity, with Roman Catholicism being the most popular. In cities particularly, religion is not as important to young people as it is to their parents and grandparents. In rural communities, though, especially among the older generation, religion is an important feature of their daily lives.

People attend Mass at the
Esztergom Basilica.

Culture, Arts, and Sports

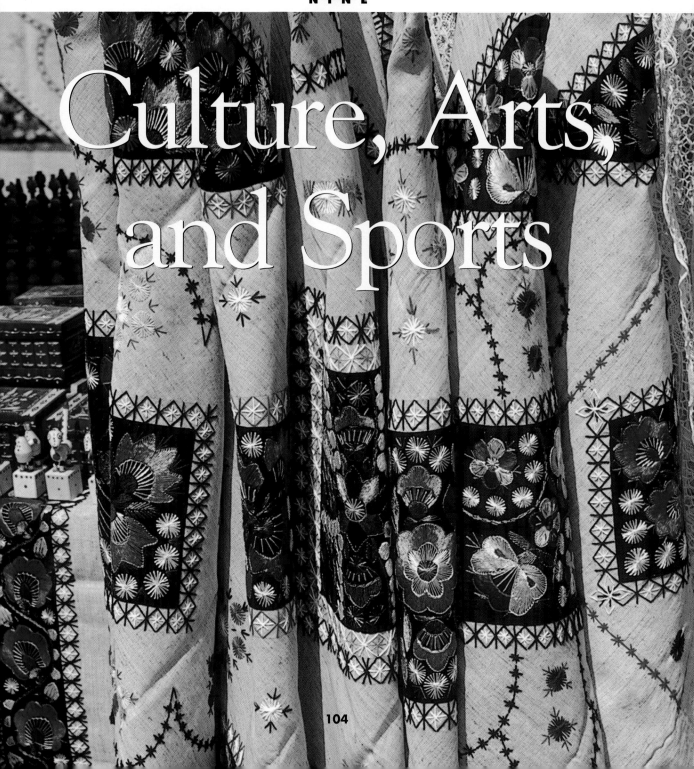

HUNGARIANS HAVE CREATED A RICH FOLK ART TRADItion. Pottery and china, made for a wide range of uses, is often covered with ornate, colorful designs featuring flowers, leaves, birds, and spirals. Wood-carvers create a wide range of objects such as flutes, penknives, pipes, and canes for local as well as tourist consumption. Most items are decorated with elaborate designs or with scenes of everyday life.

At one time, everyone made and decorated their own furniture. Peasant wives and their daughters prepared richly embroidered bride's dowries of sheets, quilts, pillows, and tablecloths. Of all of Hungary's handicrafts, women's lace

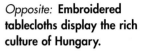

Opposite: **Embroidered tablecloths display the rich culture of Hungary.**

Pianist and Composer, Franz Liszt

Franz Liszt was born in the town of Raiding in 1811. He was taught to play the piano by his father and first performed publicly when he was only nine. A gifted musician, he was sent to study in Vienna. His compositions include piano concertos and symphonies. His most famous composition, the *Hungarian Rhapsodies*, is based on Hungarian Gypsy music. He often referred to himself as half Gypsy because of his affinity to their music. The work of Beethoven and Schubert greatly influenced him, and he arranged some of their compositions for piano. He in turn influenced the work of such younger musicians as Brahms and Grieg, as well as his son-in-law, Richard Wagner.

making and colorful embroidery are best known. Nevertheless, Hungary's greatest contributions to the arts have been in the area of music.

Music

For centuries, music has been an important part of Hungarian life. Most celebrations include folk music and dancing. In the Middle Ages, the nobility invited musicians to their courts to perform and compose. Cities and large towns today frequently have their own symphony or chamber orchestras. Musicals, folk dance programs, and ballets are often staged at cultural centers. The Hungarian State Folk Ensemble appears worldwide.

During spring, summer, and autumn, cultural festivals are common in towns both large and small. For visitors the *táncház*, dance house, is a wonderful place to experience folk music and traditional dance. Gypsy orchestras and singers entertain in many restaurants.

Three composers, in particular, are world famous. Franz Liszt was a prominent pianist and composer during the 1800s. Béla Bartók was one of the greatest composers of the 1900s. Equally famous, Zoltán Kodály based his compositions on Hungarian folk music. Although

Members of the Hungarian State Folk Ensemble perform a wedding dance.

Béla Bartók and Zoltán Kodály

Born in Transylvania in 1881, Bartók (above) studied the piano besides composition. Like Liszt, he was intensely interested in Hungarian folk music, and he and fellow composer Zoltán Kodály traveled to small villages and settlements to record folk tunes. Village elders sang to them, and they recorded the songs on wax cylinders—the forerunners of records—thus preserving a vanishing tradition. Both artists saw these melodies as a true representation of the Hungarian soul and both incorporated the tunes into their compositions. It should be kept in mind that folk music is quite different in sound from Gypsy music. The main instruments are violins, zithers, bagpipes, hurdy-gurdies, and lutes played on a five-note scale.

Kodály (right) made music readily available to the public. He spread an appreciation of Hungarian music throughout the country and became Hungary's favorite composer. Bartók's music is both individual and innovative, and today, of the two, Bartók is most popular. In 1940 Bartók emigrated to the United States, and five years later he died there, a poor man. In the repressive 1950s when Bartók's music was banned in his homeland, young people played his recordings as a political protest. In the 1970s his name became an adjective—anyone interested in peasant art was a bartóki person. In 1988 when his remains were returned to Hungary, he was accorded the status of a national hero.

Hungary had produced a number of outstanding writers, poets, and playwrights, few are known in translation outside the country. Popular plays might be by Shakespeare, Ibsen, or the dramas of modern Hungarian playwrights. Today, young Hungarians enjoy discos and clubs and follow popular trends. Since the 1960s internationally known rock bands and singers, as well musical shows, have been imported from America.

Literature

One of the earliest, and best known, pieces of Hungarian literature is the *Gesta Hungarorum*. Written between 1282 and 1285 by Simon Kézai, court cleric of King Ladislas IV, it is a fictionalized account of the Magyars' migration to what is now Hungary, and their settlement and development there.

When, in the 1500s, Bálint Balassi began writing lyric poetry, he was the first poet to write in Hungarian instead of Latin. Along with the work of Janus Pannonius, who was writing at about the same time, Bálint's work helped poetry to become an important form of literature. During the Turkish occupation in the sixteenth and seventeenth centuries, poets used their lyric words as a means of passing news from one end of the country to the other.

In the nineteenth century much of the poetry was of a style known as Romanticism, and Sándor Petfi became world famous for his romantic poems. He created new poetry techniques and widened the range of subjects that poetry could be written about. His poems celebrated patriotism and folklore as well as the joys and sorrows of ordinary people's

Ferenc Molnár, Internationally Renowned Playwright

Ferenc Molnár was born in Budapest in 1878. Although he had studied law in Switzerland, his passion was in the theater. His first play was published in 1901. During communism Molnár's plays were banned and he was almost forgotten. In present-day Hungary there is renewed interest in his work. His plays deal with themes that are meaningful to people everywhere—jealousy, for instance, and the relationship between men and women. His plays have been translated into more than twenty-five languages. In 1908 his play *The Devil* played in three different languages in four New York theaters at the same time.

Although Molnár's plays have been performed in many countries, his work was most successful in the United States, where he settled in 1939. Many plays are based on his own life. His most famous work may be *Liliom*, which became the 1945 Rogers and Hammerstein musical, *Carousel*. *The Play's the Thing*, *The Wolf*, and *The Guardsmen* have all been performed by some of the world's finest actors.

lives. Petfi had found a way for poets to express their feelings about the politics of their time.

Somewhere between 1815 and 1821 József Katona wrote Hungary's national play, *Bánk Bán*, the first great Hungarian drama. Following World War II, and through the 1950s, many novelists and playwrights were silenced by political pressure. A number of them were imprisoned to stop them from expressing their anticommunist opinions. Their brave outspokenness gave the Hungarian people the courage to rebel. The 1956 rebellion failed, however, and the artists fled the country.

In the 1960s the government loosened its tight control. Then, in 1989, constitutional changes gave the people complete artistic freedom. The voices of poets were heard again, and prose began to appear, too. In October 2002 Hungarian literature won the highest of all honors when Imre Kertész received the Nobel Prize in literature for his body of work. He was already well known for his first book, *Fateless*, one of the most devastating novels ever written about the Holocaust.

Film and Theater

Hungarians love the theater in any form, and a large number of people attend on a regular basis. Twenty-two major theaters offer seasons that run from September through early July. Open-air theaters take their place during the summer months. Some theaters specialize in opera, comedy, or musicals. Tickets are inexpensive for all kinds of performances, making it possible for people of all income levels to enjoy movies and live theater.

Theater goers in front of Budapest's Operette Theatre

Hungarians are enthusiastic moviegoers. Many films are produced within the country, but others are imported and Hungarian dialogue is dubbed in. The first Hungarian film ever produced was a documentary shot in 1901. Today there are Hungarian films on all manner of subjects, including documentaries. During communism, the film industry had a surprising amount of freedom and many films were outspoken and critical of the regime. In the 1980s István Szabó was the most prominent director in Hungary. In 1981 his film *Mephisto*, won an Oscar. The film industry was in financial trouble, so Szabó coproduced movies with other Western European studios. This brought his films, and the political problems of his country, to the attention of international audiences.

Art

Since Hungary was occupied by outsiders for such long stretches in its history, it never developed a national art style and its art is not well-known outside the country. However, the powerful post-expressionist paintings of József Rippl-Rónai brought Hungarian art into the modern world in the early twentieth century. Then, from 1946 to 1988, literature and art were forced to reflect communist ideals.

Communist control was exerted through censorship. All creative works had to be approved by party authorities before they could be presented to the public. Literature told of workers working harder under communism, and paintings showed strong, heroic workers holding the communist flag high. Massive, powerful workers or party leaders appeared in both paintings and sculptures.

In 1993 Szobon Park (a sculpture park) opened. It contained fifty-eight of the sculptures produced during communist rule. People no

Sculptures of Vladimir Lenin, among others, displayed as communist-themed pieces.

Hungary's Museums

Hungary's many museums represent a wide range of interests: aviation, art, history, sports, flags, telephones, commerce, photography, natural history, trains, stamps, the history of arts and crafts, and more. Other museums house ecclesiastical (church-related) art. There is something here for everyone, no matter what your interests.

All museums have special exhibits in October, museum month. Several villages were preserved as living museums so that visitors can see how Hungarians lived and worked centuries ago. The Open Air Village

Museum at Opusztaszer in the Tisza River region has a fisherman's hut, windmills, farmhouses, sheep pens, a narrow-gauge railway, a marketplace, and an exhibition of carriages. As visitors walk down the streets and explore the buildings, it is as if time had stood still.

longer wanted them as the focal points of public squares, or in front of government buildings, but they do represent a cultural and political era, so the park was created. In recent years, now that subject matter and style are no longer controlled by the government, a large number of street artists, including musicians, have appeared.

Sports and Recreation

With Hungary's miles of rivers and large number of lakes, it is inevitable that such water sports as swimming, boating, fishing, canoeing, water polo, and kayaking would be popular. Swimming and kayak racing are competitive sports. Other popular sports are archery, fencing, boxing, and motorcycle racing. Recently, chess has also become a spectator sport.

Hungary defends its goal at the 2003 Water Polo World League game in Budapest.

For many years the focus remained on typical Hungarian sports, whereas what were called American sports were neglected. In recent years Hungarians have become more interested in spectator sports, and soccer is enormously popular. Hungarian athletics are directed by the National Office for Physical Education and Sports. Every town has governing bodies that coordinate training and arrange sports sites.

Erno Rubik and his world-famous cube

Rubik's Cube, a small multicolored block of moveable pieces, was invented in 1975 by Erno Rubik, a Hungarian professor. From 1980 to 1983 thousands of people worldwide became obsessed with trying to solve this tantalizing and almost unsolvable puzzle. Even today there are a number of Web sites giving directions on how to solve it.

The Match of the Century

Soccer is Hungary's most popular sport and people still talk about what they call the match of the century. In 1953, at Wembley Stadium in England, the Mighty Magyars beat England 6–3, making it the first time the English had lost to a Continental team on home ground. Most of the credit for the win was given to Ferenc Puskas (right), an Olympic gold medalist.

Puskas holds the world record for the number of goals scored in a World Cup final, scoring even more goals than Brazil's great Pelé. So skillful a player was Puskas that he earned the nicknames Left-Foot Magician, Little Cannon, and Galloping Major. Although six months later Hungary again beat England in a World Cup match, they lost to West Germany in the final.

International Sports

Hungary is a strong competitor in all types of international competitions and has broken world records in archery, boxing, and motorcycle racing. Considerable emphasis is placed on the Summer Olympic Games. Hungary has competed in all but two of the Summer Games since 1896. It ranks eighth in the world in the total number of medals won. A Hungarian, Dr. Ferenc Kemény, was one of the founding members of the International Olympic Committee.

In the 2000 Sydney Olympics the Hungarian team won eight gold medals, six silver medals, and three bronze medals. Two of the gold and two of the silver medals were for kayaking. In the 2004 Summer Olympics in Athens, Greece, Hungary won a total of eighteen medals. Hungary ranked thirteenth out of 201 participating nations.

Hungary's Many Spas

Since there are over 500 of them, you can't go far in Hungary without encountering a spa of some kind. Many of them have very grand architecture. Water temperatures range between 95°F and 195°F (35°C and 91°C).

Centuries ago Celtic settlers and Roman invaders chose their sites according to the location of hot springs. The Roman regional capital, Aquincum, was near present-day Budapest. Aquincum means "lots of water." The Roman baths had floor-and-wall heating as well as canals for channeling the water.

Centuries later, the Magyars discovered the health benefits of the water. King Stephen I even built a hospital at the location of one of the springs. Other rulers added baths, but the Turks developed the many spa areas that exist today.

For centuries, tourists have come to Hungary to "take the cure," as it is called. Some spas advertise themselves as being beneficial in treating such specific ailments as arthritis. Mud cures are available at others. Spas are popular as meeting places, for relaxation, and for soaking away aches and pains. In some spas the sexes are separated, but not in all. In others, it is even possible to play chess on boards that are fixed at water level.

The warm waters of Hungary's spas are considered therapeutic.

Everyday Living

HUNGARIANS ARE HOSPITABLE, WELL-MANNERED PEOPLE. When adult guests arrive, no matter what the time of day, they are immediately offered a drink of pear, plum, or apricot brandy. It's to be drunk in one swallow, and it would be rude to refuse. If you are there for a meal, you won't leave hungry. Hungarian food is rich, hearty, and satisfying.

Most grocery shopping is done at the *piac*, or market, and since Hungarians prefer fresh ingredients, women usually shop every day. From Monday to Saturday morning, carrying baskets and bags, women shop in large market halls or outdoors in market squares. Table upon table is laden with fruit and vegetables, cheese, eggs, meat, and fish. In rural areas it is common to see women selling their own home-grown vegetables. In cities and large towns, most vegetables have been purchased from growers.

Finding the best quality and the greatest bargains takes time. Since more and more women have full-time jobs, supermarkets are popping up everywhere. For those interested in speed rather than quality and freshness, then that's the place to shop.

Opposite: **Open-air markets are a part of everyday living in Hungary.**

Favorite Foods

Traditionally, the midday meal is the main meal of the day. For many it is eaten at school or in a cafeteria at work. Most Hungarian meals start with a light vegetable soup or one made with beef or chicken broth. Cold fruit soup, a Hungarian specialty, is usually made from apples. Milk or sour cream is added. A substantial meat dish follows, often flavored with paprika, the beloved red spice common in Hungarian recipes. Pork is the most popular meat. Supper is usually leftovers—a soup, cold meats, fresh bread, peppers, and tomatoes.

Weekend meals are often quite large. When guests come, several meat dishes may be served one after the other. Stuffed cabbage, roast pig or duck, and *lecsó* (a hearty stew of red, green, or yellow peppers, and thinly sliced chorizo sausage) are all popular dishes. However, paprika-flavored *guluások* (we know it as goulash) is the dish that everyone most associates with Hungarian cooking. Sometimes goulash has the consistency of a stew but often it is more like soup. In some restaurants a mini cauldron is placed on the table and kept warm over a flame, a reminder of the days in the distant past when it was first invented and cooked in a large pot over an open fire.

A Hungarian chef shows off his goulash.

Eating Out

People rarely eat in restaurants unless it's a special occasion, although they do enjoy going out for pastries and extremely strong espresso coffee or some other kind of drink. Pastry shops, *cukrászda*, are filled to the brim with a huge variety of creamy cakes and poppy seed pastries. For a tasty snack, crêpes filled with nuts, jam, powdered chocolate, or syrup are sold at outdoor stands in parks and resorts.

Hungary has long had its own versions of fast food. A popular snack food is *lángos*, balls of deep-fried potato dough topped with sour cream and grated cheese. Sausage, fried fish, and corn on the cob are also popular. Young people enjoy getting together for hamburgers (*hamburgerek*) and hot dogs (*hotdogok*) in an American fast food restaurant.

Paprika and Goulash

When people think of Hungarian food, they think first of goulash and the spice that gives it its characteristic reddish color, paprika. Both are enduring symbols of Hungarian cuisine. Paprika—ground dried red pepper—is used in most Hungarian cooking. Fresh peppers, also known as paprika, are available in many colors and shapes. Often more than one type of pepper is used in a dish. Oddly, the pepper from which paprika is ground refuses to grow anywhere but Hungary!

Paprika was first used in the sixteenth century as a food preservative. The spices brought all the way from Asia that the wealthy used to preserve food were too costly for poorer citizens. Gradually paprika's popularity spread to all social levels and by the middle of the twentieth century it was an essential ingredient in Hungarian cooking.

Red peppers are harvested and then hung to dry before they are ground into paprika.

Goulash

Ingredients:

1 3/4 pounds beef or pork, cut into small cubes

2–3 tablespoons oil

2 finely chopped onions

1 tablespoon paprika

1 pinch caraway seeds

1 clove garlic, crushed

Salt to taste

In a frying pan, sauté the onion in heated oil. Sprinkle with caraway seeds and salt. Add the beef and brown well. Cover and lower heat. Steam for a few minutes. Add paprika and stir well. Add a little water and bring to a boil. Lower the heat again. When the meat is three-quarters cooked, add the crushed garlic. Simmer, covered, on medium heat until the meat is tender (approximately two hours), adding a little water from time to time.

Serve with potatos or noodles and a green vegetable.

The word goulash comes from *gulyasok*, cowherd, and the delicious rustic stew they made using potatoes, beef, and paprika. Many believe the dish dates back to the Magyar tribes who invented it out of necessity when they were raiding and plundering. Meat and onions were cooked together and then dried. Later, using a large pot hung over an open flame, liquid was added and the result was a hearty, nourishing "instant" soup.

Today's cooks make many versions of goulash, but the dish always includes paprika and onions plus meat—beef, pork, chicken, lamb, or even wild boar, a Hungarian specialty. It is served with potatoes, noodles, or small dumplings, *galuska*. When sour cream is added, the result is *paprikás*, a thicker, richer type of goulash. Another popular paprika dish is *lecsó*, stewed tomatoes, onions, peppers (paprika), and sausages. Sometimes scrambled eggs are added.

Life Under Communism and Life Today

The ideals of communism was a concept in which major resources and means of production are owned by the community rather than by individuals. This provided equal sharing of work, based on ability, and benefits, according to need. Instead of living healthy, comfortable lives, adults ended up working harder and living in small, run-down apartments. Since many items were unavailable, people learned to trade or barter for things they needed. Materials were traded for service. Although supplies and money have become more plentiful, people still find ways to exchange services or help each other in a communal way.

Although people were unhappy under communism, they came to rely on free medical care, guaranteed employment, and vacations organized by their employer. Entertainment was highly organized, too. Every small village had a House of Culture, but programs tended to educate rather than entertain.

Today's Hungarians still work extremely hard and expect the state to provide for them. Salaries are small, and adults are uncomfortable with those who live better lives than they do. Following communism, people regained their privacy, a privacy that is guarded fiercely. Although adults prefer an evening at home with friends to an organized activity like a club or the theater, young people like to go out whenever possible. Houses of Culture are now used for of all kinds of classes, including yoga and art, like community centers in American towns.

Housing

In the United States barn-raising parties were once common. In Hungary there is an old house-raising custom, *kaláka*. In rural areas, an extended family or a whole village might build a house together. Using weekends and spare time, the project could take many months to complete. Although popular

In rural Hungary, homes, a church, and shops make up small villages.

during communism when building materials were scarce, today the custom has almost died out.

In rural areas, villages consist of a cluster of houses, a church, post office, school, and several small shops. Geese and chickens roam the streets. Families live in stucco-covered houses with tiled or thatched roofs. Houses are often built around a small patio or vegetable gardens. Few windows face the street. High fences provide even more privacy. Home furnishings are usually simple, but brightly colored rugs and decorated plates often hang on the walls.

On the fringes of towns and cities, many families live in large apartment complexes that have shops and other services. These groups of identical buildings house small apartments that are all alike. Workers often have long commutes to reach their jobs. It is impossible for most people to afford anything better. The hostels where factory workers live are crowded and shabby. An estimated 30,000 Hungarians are homeless.

For years, most property was government-owned, but now some middle-class Hungarians are able to purchase narrow plots of land outside towns. Often doing the construction themselves, families build tiny weekend houses. Some people even take on second and third jobs to make this possible.

Education

Hungary has come a long way in the field of education. Today, Hungary has one of the highest literacy rates in Europe. Whether they live in towns or villages, most children attend kindergarten from age three through six. Attendance is not enforced. Compulsory education begins at age seven. Parents are urged to be involved in their children's education either during the day or with the many after-school activities.

From age ten onward, students usually learn two foreign languages, English and German. As adults, both languages will be necessary for opportunities in international business. Often there is also a year or more of French, Italian, or

Primary schools are filled with students aged three to six, though attendance is not mandatory at this young age.

Spanish instruction. Latin was taught until the middle of the twentieth century. The Hungarian language (Magyar) and the Hungarian constitution are studied. Other subjects are much the same as in other countries— math, science, geography, history, art, gymnastics, and music. Considerable emphasis is placed on scientific subjects. Music instruction is based on a successful system developed by the famed composer Zoltán Kodály.

Hopscotch

Most people know the child's game of hopscotch, but they may not be aware it is played so many different ways worldwide. For example, hopscotch played in the United States has different rules and a slightly different design from the one played in England. Hungarian hopscotch looks totally different from either of them, and the rules are quite different. It takes both concentration and good balance. Here is how to play it.

With a piece of chalk draw a big spiral on the ground. Divide the spiral into squares. Fifteen or sixteen squares is a good number. The more squares you have, the longer the game will last. Number the squares with the first outside square being number one. Your spiral will look like a snail shell.

The first player hops on one leg from number one to the last inside square. He can rest on the center square before hopping all the way out. If he puts his foot down, or touches a line, his turn is over. If he succeeds in hopping into all of the squares, he turns his back and throws a small stone onto the spiral. Wherever it lands is his "house." He is the only one who can step in that square. At the end, the winner is the one who has the most houses. Try it! It's a challenging variation of a popular game.

Secondary Schools, Colleges . . . and Vacations

Students may leave school when they are sixteen, but most Hungarian teenagers choose to continue. There are two types of secondary school. The *gimnazium* has a traditional academic program. The vocational trade school is known as a *technikum*. Students who attend a technikum learn a trade or skill. Some factories and farms also have specialized training schools.

Teens attend science class.

When secondary school is completed, the youth has a choice of eighty-nine institutions of higher learning. There are thirty state-run universities and colleges, twenty-six church-affiliated universities and colleges, as well as six colleges run by foundations. Of the existing universities, three specialize in technical subjects, six in medicine, six are agricultural, and five focus on the arts. The first university opened in Pécs in 1367. University entrance is extremely competitive and few students are able to attend. The majority of degrees awarded are in various areas of science.

Summer vacation lasts from mid-June to September and many boys attend camps in the mountains or on Lake Balaton. Swimming (often in thermally heated water), hiking, and cycling are popular in the summer months with ice-skating and soccer taking their place in winter. Adults enjoy hunting large birds or hares in the forests and marshes along the Danube and Tisza rivers.

Festivals and Holidays

Prior to communism, traditional festivals and holidays followed both religious and agricultural calendars. Saints' days, planting, and harvesting days were all celebrated with joy and ceremony. Communism replaced these familiar celebrations with political holidays that commemorated important events in communist

Cultural, Political, and Religious Holidays

New Year's Day	January 1
Revolution Day	March 15
Easter Monday	April
Labor Day	May 1
Whitsun Monday	May
National Day/Saint Stephen's Day	August 20
Republic Day	October 23
Remembrance Day	November 1
Christmas	December 25 and 26

history. Large numbers of people (often children) were forced to participate in massive parades. When communism ended, the centuries-old traditional holidays were restored, with March 15, 1848, Revolution Day, being the only holiday common to both calendars. Today it celebrates patriotism. October 23, another national holiday, recalls the martyrs and victims of the communist era and the 1956 uprising.

In villages and farming communities, celebrations are a mix of religion and ancient agricultural traditions. Easter customs date back to pagan times. In the country, boys call on girls, sprinkling them with water; in cities, they use perfume. Girls give the boys eggs decorated with elaborate folk art designs, or small amounts of money. Easter feasts include boiled eggs and ham.

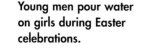

Young men pour water on girls during Easter celebrations.

Outdoor harvest festivals in August and September involve eating, drinking, singing, and folk dancing. Annual fairs, with folk dancing and folk music, are an opportunity for craftspeople to exhibit and sell their work.

In a custom that has died out, a young man set up a maypole in front of his girlfriend's house. A bunch of lilacs was fixed on top.

If the girl accepted his gift, she hung colorful ribbons from the pole. Weddings are festive events and each region has its own customs, which include regional songs and dances. Well-wishers speak their farewells to the newlyweds.

As is common in other Catholic countries, birthday celebrations occur on name days—the feast day of the saint a person is named after rather than the day on which a person was born. Many days on the calendar are named after popular saints. On days that do not honor a saint, common first names are chosen. Name days are family events celebrated with a special dinner, flowers, and the giving of small gifts. The gathering of the family is considered more important than any gift.

Kalocsa's Spice Pepper Museum

The fact that the town of Kalocsa has an entire museum devoted to paprika will give you some idea of its importance in the lives and cuisine of the Hungarian people. On display are the tools used in harvesting the peppers, such as rakes and hoes. Museum guides enthusiastically describe the different types of peppers and how they are grown, dried, and ground into paprika.

In the fertile area between Kalocsa and Szeged, paprika is the main crop. The hot, light-colored peppers grow best near Kalocsa, whereas the redder, milder peppers grow near Szeged. In September, the three-inch to five-inch-long peppers are harvested, threaded onto strings, and hung from every building to dry (right). Once dried, the peppers are sent for processing. It takes 3 pounds (1.4 kg) of dried peppers to make 1 pound (.5 kg) of ground paprika.

The pepper harvest celebration includes exhibits, sports events, conferences, and a chess tournament. The festivities culminate in a Paprika Harvest Parade in which local bands and colorful folk dance groups perform.

Timeline

Hungarian History

Compromise of 1867 establishes dual monarchy of Austria-Hungary.	1867
Archduke Francis Ferdinand, heir to Austro-Hungarian throne, assassinated, causing start of World War I.	1914
Austria-Hungary is defeated in World War I.	1914–1918
Hungarians revolt, declaring Hungary a republic; Count Mihály Károlyi becomes president.	1918
Treaty of Trianon, part of World War I peace settlement, takes away two-thirds of prewar Hungary.	1920
Hungary enters World War ll on side of Nazi Germany.	1941
Hungary signs armistice with Allies; World War II ends; Hungary forms coalition government; Hungary again declared a republic; social and economic reforms occur.	1945
Communist Party renames itself the Hungarian Socialist Party. A new National Day, March 15, observed holiday in honor of Revolution Against Austrian Rule.	1989
In elections in March and April, Hungarian Socialist Party voted out of power; a multiparty democratic government takes office; new constitution written.	1990
In new elections, Hungarian Socialist Party forms coalition government with the Alliance of Free Democrats.	1994
Hungary joins NATO.	1999
Fernc Mádl becomes president.	2000
Hungary joins European Union.	2004

World History

1865	The American Civil War ends.
1914	World War I breaks out.
1917	The Bolshevik Revolution brings communism to Russia.
1929	Worldwide economic depression begins.
1939	World War II begins, following the German invasion of Poland.
1945	World War II ends.
1957	The Vietnam War starts.
1969	Humans land on the moon.
1975	The Vietnam War ends.
1979	Soviet Union invades Afghanistan.
1983	Drought and famine in Africa.
1989	The Berlin Wall is torn down, as communism crumbles in Eastern Europe.
1991	Soviet Union breaks into separate states.
1992	Bill Clinton is elected U.S. president.
2000	George W. Bush is elected U.S. president.
2001	Terrorists attack World Trade Towers, New York, and the Pentagon, Washington, D.C.
2003	A coalition of forty-nine nations, headed by the United States and Great Britain, invade Iraq.

Fast Facts

Official name: Republic of Hungary (Magyar Köztársaság)

Capital: Budapest

Official language: Magyar (Hungarian)

Budapest

Hungary's flag

Sunflower field

Official religion:	none
National anthem:	"Himnusz" ("Hymn")
Government:	parliamentary democracy
Chief of state:	president
Head of government:	prime minister
Area:	35,919 square miles (93,030 sq km)
Greatest distances east to west:	312 miles (502 km)
Greatest distances north to south:	193 miles (311 km)
Latitude and longitude of geographic center:	47' 00' N, 20' 00' E
Bordering countries:	Croatia, Serbia and Montenegro to the south, Romania to the east, the Ukraine, and Slovakia to the north, and Austria, and Slovenia to the west
Highest elevation:	Mount Kékes, 3,330 feet (1,015 m) above sea level
Lowest elevation:	Near Szeged, 259 feet (79 m) above sea level
Average temperatures:	32°F (0°C) in January; 71°F (21.6°C) in July
Average precipitation:	26.4 inches (671 mm)
National population (2000 est.):	9,877,000

Population of largest cities (2001 est.):

Budapest	1,812,000
Debrecen	211,038
Miskolc	184,129
Szeged	168,276
Pécs	162,502

Parliament House

Currency

Famous landmarks:
- ▶ *Castle Hill*, Budapest
- ▶ *Fisherman's Bastion*, Budapest
- ▶ *Matthias Church*, Budapest
- ▶ *The Royal Palace*, Budapest
- ▶ *Parliament House*, Budapest
- ▶ *Gellért Spa Baths*, Budapest
- ▶ *Views from the Liberty Bridge*, Budapest
- ▶ *The Danube Bend region of the Danube*
- ▶ *Lake Balaton*

Industry: Hungary is Central Europe's most economially developed country. Its main products are textiles, foods, beverages, chemicals, pharmaceuticals, plastics, steel, aluminum, machinery, and transportation equipment. Its principal exports are meat (particularly spicy sausages), fruit and vegetables, wine, electrical equipment, steel, and such transportation equipment as buses and car parts.

Currency: Hungary uses the forint. In October 2004, U.S.$1 = 200.02 forints.

System of weights and measures: Hungary uses the metric system.

Literacy (1980 est.): 99.4%

Schoolgirl

Béla Bartók

Common words and phrases:

Jó napot kívánok.	Hello.
Jó reggelt.	Good morning.
Jó estét.	Good evening.
Köszönöm.	Thank you.
Hogy van?	How are you?
Hogy hívjak?	What's your name?
A nevem . . .	My name is . . .
Akarok menni . . .	I want to go to . . .
Mennyibe kerül?	How much is it?
Hol van . . . ?	Where is . . . ?

Famous Hungarians:

Béla Bartók   (1881–1945)
Composer

Zoltán Kodály   (1882–1967)
Composer

Franz Liszt   (1811–1886)
Composer

King Matthias Corvinus   (1443–1490)
Hungarian king and general

Cardinal József Mindszenty   (1892–1975)
Bishop

Ferenc Molnár   (1878–1952)
Playwright

Stephen I (Saint Stephen)   (975–1038)
First king of Hungary

To Find Out More

Fiction

▶ Seredy, Kate. *The Singing Tree*. New York: Puffin, 1990.

▶ Wiseman, Eva. *My Canary Yellow Star*. Toronto: Tundra Books, 2002.

Nonfiction

▶ *Hungary* (Fiesta series). Series 3, Volume 5. Danbury, CT: Grolier, 2004.

▶ Koras, Zsuzanna, and Molnar, Adrienne. *Carrying a Secret in My Heart: Children of the Victims of the Reprisals after the Hungarian Revolution in 1956. An Oral History.* Budapest-New York: Central European University Press, 2003.

▶ Lundrigan, Nicole. *Hungary*. Milwaukee, WI: Gareth Stevens Publishing, 2002.

▶ Popescu, Julian. *Hungary* (Major World Nations series). Broomall, PA: Chelsea House Publishers, 2000.

Web Sites

▶ **CIA World Factbook**
http://www.cia.gov/cia/publications/
factbook
*Contains statistical information such
as size, population, government,
economy, and transportation.*

▶ **Welcome to Hungary**
www.gotohungary.com/information/
*Tourism site that contains general
information on places to visit.*

▶ **Government Portal, Hungary**
http://www.magyarorszag.hu/angol
*Contains information on geographic
regions, climate, flora and fauna,
and education, among others.*

Organizations and Embassies

▶ **Hungarian Embassy**
3910 Shoemaker Street, NW
Washington, D.C. 20008
(202) 362-6730

▶ **Hungarian National Tourist Office**
150 East 58th Street
New York, NY 10155-3398
(212) 355-0240

Index

Page numbers in *italics* indicate illustrations.

government
    communist, 49–52
    constitution, 52, 55, 59–60
    executive branch, 55–56
    judicial branch, 59
    legislative branch, 56–57
    religion and, 101
Great Alföld. *see* Great Plain
Great Plain, the, 19, 20–21
Great Synagogue, 97, *97*
Grósz, Károly, 51
The Guardsmen (Molnár), 109
guluások (goulash). *see* goulash
Gypsies, 85–87

H

Hapsburg dynasty, 42–44, 93, 95
health care, 89, 115
Hitler, Adolf, 47
holidays and festivals, 125–127
hopscotch, 124
Horthy, Miklós, *46*, 47
Hortobágy National Park, 30, *31*
Hortobágy region, 30
Houses of Culture, 121
housing, 121–122
Hungarian Civic Alliance, 57
Hungarian Democratic Forum, 52, 57
Hungarian people. *see* Magyars;
    minority groups
Hungarian Socialist Party, 52, 53, 56–57,
    60. *see also* Communist Party
Hungarian Socialist Workers' Party
    (HSWP). *see* Communist Party
Hungarian State Folk Ensemble, 106, *106*
Hungarian Workers' Party, 52
Hungary
    borders of, 19, 47, 83
    maps of, *15, 41*

    origin of name, 37
    size of, 18
Hunyadi, János, 40

I

independence movement, 43, 61
industry, 49, 74–77
invasions, foreign, 12, 13, 39, *39*, 51
irrigation, 68

J

Jewish people, 84, 96–98
Josvafo (village), *25*
judicial branch, 59

K

Kádár, János, 51
kaláda (house-building), 121–122
Kalocsa Spice Pepper Museum, 127
Kányavári Island, 30
Károlyi, Mihály, Count, 46
Katona, József, 109
Kemény, Ferenc, 114
Kertész, Imre, 109–110
Kézai, Simon, 108
Khan, Batu, 39
Kiskunság National Park, 31, 32
Kodály, Zoltán, 13, 106, 107, 123
Kossuth, Lajos, 43, 44, 61, *61*
Krös-Maros National Park, 31
Kun, Béla, 46–47

L

Ladislas IV (Hungarian king), 108
Lake Balaton, 11, *23*, 23, 26
lakes and rivers, 10, 19, 23, 25–26
Lake Tisza, 30

lángos (fried dough), 118
languages
    education in, 123
    Hungarian, 83, 88, 89–91
    minority groups and, 60
    Romany, 91
lecsó (stew), 118, 120
legislative branch, 56–57
Liliom (Molnár), 109
Lipizzaner horses, *73*, 73–74
Liszt, Franz, 13, 97, 105, 106
Little Balaton, 30
liturature, 108–110
livestock, 73–74
Louis I (Hungarian king), 40

M

Mádl, Ferenc, *53*, 53, 55
Magyars, 13, 37, 38, 83, 93
manners, 88, 117
manufacturing. *see* industry
maps
    Budapest, 64
    ethnicities, 85
    foreign invasions, 39
    geographical, *18*
    Hungary, *15*, *41*, *46*
    natural resources, *75*
    population, *83*
Maria Theresa (empress of Austria),
    42, 42–43
marriage, 94, 127
Mary (Hungarian queen), 40
Mátra Mountains, 20, 25
Matthias Church, 99
Mattias Corvinus (Hungarian king),
    40, *40*
Maximilian II (Holy Roman Emperor),
    42

maypoles, 126–127
Medgyessy, Péter, 56, *56*
Mephisto (film), 110
Mindszenty, József, Cardinal, 48, 98, 101
mining, 77
Ministry of Culture, 101
minority groups, 12, 60, 84–87, 91
Miskolc, 74–75
Molnár, Ferenc, 109
Mongol invaders, 39
mountains, 17, 20, 25
Mount Kékes, 20, 25
museums, 112
    Christian Museum, 24
music and dance, 87, 106–108, 123

N

Nagy, Imre, 50, 51
name days, 127
names, 90
national anthems, 63
National Assembly, 56, 56–57
National Church Council, 101
nationalism, 44
National Office for Physical Education
    and Sports, 113
national parks, 21, 31
natural resources
    map of, *75*
    mining of, 77
    oil and gas, 21
Nazi party, 47
neighboring countries, 19, 47, 83
New Economic Mechanism, 51
nobles, 40–41
North Atlantic Treaty Organization
    (NATO), 53
Northern Highlands, 20, 25

Meet the Author

Ann Stalcup is an author and teacher. She lives in Malibu, California, but grew up in England and has also lived and worked in Vancouver, Canada. As a teacher, nothing gives her greater pleasure than introducing to elementary school students the cultures of other countries.

Stalcup loves to travel and has visited all seven continents and over one hundred countries. One summer, while visiting Eastern European countries, she spent some time in Hungary. There, she and her husband explored the countryside, sampled spicy Hungarian dishes, listened to wild Gypsy music, and walked and walked as they explored Budapest's many beautiful historic buildings. She most enjoyed resting on wooden benches while watching the river traffic on the busy Danube.

Researching today's Hungary was a fascinating experience for Stalcup. She read recently written books, accessed U.S. and Hungarian government Web sites in search of relevant information, spoke with people who had grown up in Hungary, and let guidebooks enrich her knowledge of important sites. In addition, other Web sites and books provided information on famous people, products, politics, government, religion, arts and crafts, food, and the landscape. And then it was time to write. That process was much like fitting the many pieces of a puzzle together. This is Ann Stalcup's first book for Children's Press.

Photo Credits